A Solitary Rose
by
Robert M. Oliva
(1919–1996)

ALONE in the Mainstream

A Deaf Woman Remembers
Public School

Gina A. Oliva

Gallaudet University Press
WASHINGTON, D.C.

Deaf Lives

A Series Edited by BRENDA JO BRUEGGEMANN

Gallaudet University Press
Washington, D.C. 20002
http://gupress.gallaudet.edu

Note: Though every effort was made to secure the permission of each individual pictured in this work, some names may have been omitted to protect the identities of those individuals who could not be contacted. Identifying characteristics of the survey participants have been altered in order to ensure their anonymity.

The painting *Milan, Italy, 1880* by Mary Thornley on page 7 is reprinted by permission of the painter.

Willard J. Madsen's poem "You Have to Be Deaf to Understand" on pages 171–73 is reprinted by permission of the author.

Printed in the United States of America

Library of Congress Cataloging-in-Publication Data

Oliva, Gina A.
    Alone in the mainstream : a deaf woman remembers public school / Gina A. Oliva.
        p. cm. — (Deaf lives)
    Includes bibliographical references and index.
    ISBN 1-56368-300-8 (pbk. : alk. paper)
        1. Oliva, Gina A.   2. Deaf women—United States—Biography.   3. Deaf—
Education—United States.   4. Mainstreaming in education—United States.
5. Deaf—Government policy—United States.   6. Deaf—United States—Interviews.
I. Title.   II. Series.
    HV2534.O55A3 2004
    371.91'2'092—dc22

                                                                2004043296

♾ The paper used in this publication meets the minimum requirements of American National Standard for Information Sciences—Permanence of Paper for Printed Library Materials, ANSI z39.48-1984.

To my mother Katherine Papaharris Oliva
To my father Robert Michael Oliva
For being the pioneers that they were.
To my paternal grandfather Jacob, his mother Josephine,
and all the other Olivas whom I never had the good fortune
to meet, who shared my fate of being deaf and were
presumably alone in the mainstream.

To the members of the Deaf community for their longstanding resilience, without whom I would be consigned to
always and ever live as a solitary.

To the many scholars, both deaf and hearing, who have
before me done their part in recording the struggles and
triumphs of a very special people. I am indebted to so many
of you for inspiring my thinking and direction.

And to the deaf and hard of hearing children of today
and tomorrow, all over the world: I pray that you will
always and ever have the opportunity that I have had, to
live in two worlds.

Contents

SOLITARY 1 a : being, living, or going alone or without companions **b** : saddened by isolation
2 : UNFREQUENTED, DESOLATE **3 a** : taken, passed, or performed without companions <a solitary ramble> **b** : keeping a prisoner apart from others <solitary confinement>
4 : being at once single and isolated <a solitary example>
5 a : occurring singly and not as part of a group or cluster <flowers terminal and solitary> **b** : not gregarious, colonial, social, or compound <solitary bees>

Solitaire 1 : a single gem (as a diamond) set alone

Merriam Webster's Collegiate Dictionary, Tenth Edition

Editor's Foreword

Alone and Together

Gina Oliva's *Alone in the Mainstream* inaugurates Gallaudet University Press's "Deaf Lives" series. As the opening act for a series intended to feature contemporary autobiographies and biographies written by or about "modern" deaf and hard of hearing people, Oliva's book offers us some of both related genres. In *Alone in the Mainstream,* Oliva has successfully blended autobiography and biography in creating an energized and sensitive narrative that weaves her own experiences as a (then "hard of hearing") young solitaire "mainstreamed" in "regular" public schools alongside the stories of many other solitaries (as she defines them), who were also "mainstreamed." She has gathered these stories as "data" in a biographical study she conducted and called "The Solitary Mainstream Project."

What Oliva does in melding her research with her own life, mixing analysis with autobiography, and blending personal narrative themes with the qualitative methodology of interview-based case studies should be remarkable enough. But she does even more: She also offers commentary about ways to make the "solitary mainstreamed" lives of young deaf and hard of hearing kids less solitary, more socially successful, more well-rounded.

Such commentary layered effectively in her text, makes *Alone in the Mainstream* valuable in at least two ways: First, because of its format, this text addresses a wide audience and second, it serves as an ideal model for the Deaf Lives series itself. Not only does Oliva write with a sparkling fresh "voice" that makes her text attractive to those generally interested in autobiography, but her focused subject set around the reflective stories and commentary gathered from other deaf and hard of hearing adults who were once mainstreamed, gives the book purpose, clarity, and a unique spot on the literary shelves as it appeals to multiple audiences.

To be sure, since the implementation of the Individuals with Disabilities Education Act (IDEA) there have been studies of mainstreaming and its effects that have been completed not only on deaf and hard of hearing children but also on children with disabilities. Oliva mentions Michelle Yetmen's study in this area, and Susan Foster's research primarily in the 1980s; both generally point to the same "catch-22" pattern that concerns Oliva's fifth chapter: That mainstreamed deaf and hard of hearing children by and large experience—and report having experienced—elevated academic opportunities while "in the mainstream," while they also report social isolation, sometimes extreme, in this educational setting. Yet, Oliva's book is the first that I know of to report this experience from an "adult" point of view. And as Oliva herself makes clear, the power of these adult experiences to serve as models—even as mentors, she hopes—for future generations of mainstreamed deaf lives is no small power.

Deaf Lives leading deaf lives then—this move is the second major significance of *Alone in the Mainstream*. And it is the move that also makes it the ideal book for opening a series aimed at doing just that—letting deaf lives, in their infinite and interesting variety, lead other deaf lives, surely also in infinite and interesting variety. (And along the way, others who are not deaf or hard of hearing—like the parents, teachers, siblings, and peers that Oliva frequently addresses in her commentary—might also "listen in" or "read over the shoulders" too.) The series was conceived with the hope of simply offering a space where more deaf lives could be written and read so that other deaf lives could read them, know them, perhaps even come to write alongside them (just as Oliva's "subjects" came to write alongside each other in her themed chapters). And again, a good number of others are bound to enjoy—and benefit from—learning from and about such books as well.

In fact, Oliva's book is not just the opening act in the series, but in some ways it actually opened the door to the series. Oliva's manuscript came in first as a regular submission to the Gallaudet University Press editorial board, before the Deaf Lives series was invented. All who read the manuscript immediately saw the multiple values in it—in the fresh, engaging voice Oliva writes in, in her attempt to blend personal narrative with interview-based qualitative research, and in the need to have the effects of "mainstreaming" explored by adults who had long since been through the process. But the manuscript also did not fit well within the corpus of Gallaudet University Press's other books: It was not entirely historical biography, not entirely memoir/autobiography, and not entirely academic research. It fell between many cracks.

At the same time, the press was struggling with several other crack-dwelling books that involved autobiography. It seemed a shame to let these deaf lives slip between the publication cracks and so I suggested to the press that perhaps they might "break off" most of the autobiographical (and some nonhistorical biographical) manuscripts they received and use them to form a new series, akin to the already successful sociolinguistics series headed by Ceil Lucas. It was an idea whose time was ripe—*kairotic*, as the ancient Greeks called an idea and discursive exchange whose moment in time and place was "just right." And so, Deaf Lives was born with Oliva's text.

Met deaf wow!

I waited eleven years later than Gina Oliva to make a journey to the "deaf-world." I was thirty-one years old when I first came to Gallaudet University, having been mainstreamed in a rural western Kansas school in the era—just like Oliva—before mainstreaming became official with Public Law 94–142 and IDEA. The similarities do not stop there.

Although I have not stayed at Gallaudet University, nor do I make my daily work within the sphere of the Deaf community (as a professor of English, Women's Studies, and Comparative Studies at Ohio State University), much of my own experience and my ways of operating in the world seemed to be of a piece with those Oliva often describes. I learned early, as Oliva did, how to "cope" and adjust my communication strategies to fit or follow the cues (or merely mock those) of hearing people I was in contact with. I have spent a fair amount of my own scholarly and personal writing time compelled to "answer back" to a parent—although I aimed for my mother while Oliva's focus was her father. I have experienced the great discomfort of being pedestaled—celebrated by (usually unknowing) hearing acquaintances for my perceived superiority in not being like "them" ("them" being whatever notion my acquaintances had gripped in their heads about the limits of deaf people). Disclosure—the fear of it, the negotiation of it, the anxiety of it, the freedom of it—has preoccupied much of my life as I have "passed," then simultaneously pondered the consequences of passing, refused to pass, and too, celebrated the potential productive space of being "in passing." I too have longed for positive deaf (and female and professional) role models and lamented the lack of such role models for the young deaf and hard of hearing kids I come into contact with now, almost all mainstreamed. I've counted reading as my refuge for most of my life—and have written (and read!) passionately about this literate refuge in most of my academic and personal essays. I've stayed ever busy, looking almost always "just fine" and intensely occupied in what I was doing since then the chances of random social conversations are reduced. In my adult life, I've found myself deeply engaged in things "sporty"—although I was never much of an athlete during my school years, either—and I have been drawn in particular to the kinds of sports that involved little talking but occurred in close contact and somewhat social spaces that would maximize my abilities to "hear" and also make me more likely an "equal" without overburdening my listening abilities: running, biking, racquetball, swimming, and now Tae Kwon Do. And finally, I've been working a lot lately to expend my own spheres of interest and abilities in ways that might benefit deaf and hard of hearing kids: mentoring several of them at Ohio State University; starting the American Sign Language (ASL) program at Ohio State; fostering an ASL club at a nearby public elementary school (they have ASL classes during the lunch hour during the winter when the kids stay in from recess); and instigating a Tae Kwon Do class for deaf and hard of hearing teenagers in central Ohio.

I do these things for most of the same reasons Oliva does: to work toward changing the huge social-academic gap in the experience of today's mainstreamed deaf and hard of hearing children, to offer them multiple positive role models, to thrill in the "metdeafwow" experience, and finally, to further educate and illustrate to the peers, teachers, and parents of these deaf and hard of hearing kids with enormous potential that perhaps they really do not have to grow up "alone in the mainstream."

For More Than Deaf Eyes . . .

But *Alone in the Mainstream* is about more than just meeting other deaf people; it is also about the needed bridge between deaf and hearing people over the potential of future deaf children. It is then, for more than just deaf eyes—a point Oliva makes herself in her concluding chapters.

In winter 2002, I taught a first-ever "special topics" class in the Ohio State University English Department: English 575: Representations of Deafness in Literature and Film. One of the students in that class was Lauren Kelley, a student who had become my advisee and with whom I had the pleasure of sharing two other English courses with already. During this particular course, twenty Ohio State University students majoring in English were online with eighteen students enrolled in Professor Susan Burch's "American Deaf History" course at Gallaudet University. The two groups of students shared a Web-based discussion space daily, and they also had one shared assignment—to view and respond to a documentary on cochlear implants, *Sound and Fury,* that was being aired on PBS that same winter. (Burch and I came to call this shared exchange between our students, "The Flying Words Project," in honor of our mutual favorite American Sign Language poet, Peter Cook.) Having expressed deep interest in deaf women's autobiographical accounts during the first few weeks of the course, I gave Lauren a copy of Gina Oliva's early manuscript and asked for her comments on it. In the end, Lauren became a kind of co-editor with me for this particular manuscript and she also made it the subject of a conference presentation at the Multiple Perspectives on Disability conference in April 2003, as well as the focus of her final project in another later course (fall 2003), Introduction to Disability Studies. Here Lauren Kelley offers her summary reading and sensitive interpretation of Oliva's text through nondeaf eyes.

• • •

Oliva's manuscript is autobiographical and biographical, containing her stories and the stories of others who were mainstreamed into hearing schools, as deaf and hard of hearing students. Immediately, Oliva creates a connection between the words "solitary" and "solitaire." She cites the definition of the former as "secluded, lonely," and the latter "a diamond or other gemstone set alone, as in a ring." After making this connection, Oliva often refers to the deaf individuals who were mainstreamed as "solitaires." This term *solitaires* captures the tensions between the isolated loneliness of those mainstreamed in the past, with Oliva's glittering hope for those mainstreamed in the future. Likewise, as her terminology suggests, their isolation as children was not because they lacked worth, but rather because others did not accept and accommodate their difference and because others did not see their difference as a distinguishing beauty. In this way, she explains that a major aspiration for writing her book is to reevaluate representations of the past, showing them from another perspective. She does so by connecting the experiences of these seeming loners together, creating a powerful voice and community.

Gina grew up in Cos Cob, Connecticut, with a family that—despite her father and sister's hearing loss—acknowledges her deafness in the simple phrase "just can't hear too well." In kindergarten, at the Cos Cob School, Gina's difference from the other children becomes apparent for the first time when she cannot follow instructions based on music. Because of her inability to hear the music, she is left sitting alone, singled out, and deeply embarrassed. As she gets older, Gina relies on "noticing visual cues" and "copying other's actions" to avoid embarrassing situations and to compensate for her impairment, as she suggests deaf people often do. And yet interaction with her hearing classmates, because of her difference, is "increasingly problematic" (21). "That difference," she writes, "colored, overshadowed, permeated, and consumed every single school day of my life" (21).

In sharing their stories of isolation and loneliness as children, these deaf adults discover—along with the reader—that they are not alone in their experiences, as Oliva connects the stories that share similar sentiments and commonalties. For example, as children, many of the "solitaires" dreaded disclosing their hearing loss to others. This dread demonstrates that there was a particular shame that they felt about their deafness, which made them uncomfortable with talking about it and often lead to attempts in hiding it. But the "solitaires" did not create this shame—it was forced on them by those around them. Many "solitaires," after disclosing (intentionally or unintentionally), had stories of being teased and not accepted. Oliva, similarly, grows up in an environment where her impairment is not openly discussed. Every morning her mother pins her hair in a manner that hides her hearing aid. This simple action reinforces (every single day) that deafness is something to hide. But the problem with hiding this truth, Oliva recognizes, is that "lack of disclosure permits, enables, and perpetuates the invisibility of deafness" (73). And in perpetuating this invisibility, it is difficult for either deaf or hearing to become comfortable with the idea of hearing loss. Because of this lack of acceptance, deafness remains a reason to be teased, feel shame, and to have difficulties coming to terms with a deaf identity. By exposing these resulting issues, Oliva encourages her readers to challenge past conventions, and to rethink them for the future.

It is not until Gina is in college and is exposed to sign language that she becomes comfortable disclosing her deafness. She begins to study deaf children and their education. When she is twenty, she makes the decision to enter the "Deaf world" (22). As she states, "Over the next few decades, I learned a new way of living . . . my life became full, vibrant and satisfying; I could function at my full potential" (22–23). Because of Gina's success with sign language and in the deaf community, paired with her many frustrations among people with hearing, the reader cannot help but wonder if mainstreaming deaf children is a mistake. This question looms throughout the entire book, sometimes more obvious and ominous than at other times. And yet there is not a simple answer. As Oliva writes, "participants were generally satisfied with their *academic* experience, declaring, 'It made me who I am.'" (74). The issue that remains, however, is the one explored most deeply in her central chapter (5) and again in the last two chapters: how to make this successful academic experience also successful socially.

A New World

I began reading deaf autobiography in Professor Brenda Brueggemann's Deafness and Literature class. As a hearing student, I was entering a kind of uncharted territory; to me, it was a new world. When the class was over, I kept reading because I wanted to keep learning. Too often, it seems, we learn about others from a third-party source, instead of from the direct written or spoken (or signed!) account from the people themselves. I was fascinated with this group of people—deaf and hard of hearing people—whom I had never really thought much about before, and became interested in their experiences in a society that is predominately hearing. I was struck by similar resonations and reoccurrences among these vastly unique individuals, especially their isolation when language barriers negatively impact companionship.

As readers of earlier versions of Oliva's book, two of us (one hearing and in her twenties, the other hard of hearing and in her forties) came together to recognize *Alone in the Mainstream* as a carefully crafted culmination of the commonalities—and distinctions—among deaf children mainstreamed into a hearing environment. It is a candid and honest view of the mainstreamed child's experience, from an adult perspective. When we finished reading the text, we were both struck with the realization of the many different groups of people—regardless of hearing ability—that this book has the potential to benefit. True, this is foremost a book for the "solitaires" themselves who, because of this opportunity, are able to share and document their stories. This is a book that creates a space for them to connect as adults even though they were not able to as children.

But beyond the "solitaires" themselves this is also a book for hearing parents with a deaf child, as that child—part of the next generation—

needs a support system to avoid being "alone" themselves. "Many of the informants," Oliva explains, "even those who said they would choose to be mainstreamed again feel that their loneliness could have been lessened if those around them had been more aware of how to help" (75). In this way, finally (and most importantly), this is a book for everyone else! For it is those who actually make up the mainstream that determine—by their willingness, understanding, acceptance, and awareness—what a main-streamed child's experience will be.

BRENDA JO BRUEGGEMANN AND LAUREN KELLEY

ALONE in the Mainstream

INTRODUCTION

"I was the only one." I have heard this comment over and over again during my thirty years at Gallaudet University. In the course of conversation with other deaf or hard of hearing adults, we would shortly discover that we had both spent our K–12 years as the single deaf or hard of hearing child in a regular school. Invariably, we were drawn to each other. Invariably, we would share common experiences: "Oh yes, I know exactly what you mean," and "That happened to me too," and "I never realized there were other hard of hearing kids going through the same thing!"

I was the only child with a hearing loss in all the schools I attended during my K–12 and college years, at least to the best of my knowledge. This experience of being the solitary child "made me who I am," to use the words of several of the deaf and hard of hearing adults who contributed to this book. I entered kindergarten in 1954 with a 50-dB loss and graduated from high school in 1968 with a 75-dB loss.[1] This is considered a moderate-to-severe loss, and with hearing aids, I could hear people who spoke directly to me. Without the hearing aids, I was deaf, for all practical purposes.

Although my father had a hearing loss, and one of my sisters does as well, our family did not do anything special to accommodate us. We didn't use the word "deaf" to describe ourselves. We just "couldn't hear too well." During my school years, my father and I never discussed the hearing loss; my mother and I discussed it only when I came home from school in tears.

Fortunately, both of my parents were avid readers, and I seem to have inherited their love for learning. I was a bookworm from the word go and always did well in school because of that—lucky for me because the schools did not provide any special services. As far as they were concerned, I was just like everybody else. These were the years before federal legislation, but, for all intents and purposes, I lived through what now is known as *mainstreaming*, or more specifically, *inclusion*. Beginning in the third grade, I began to see that my social involvement with other kids was somehow lacking. This awareness, not only of my limited social circle but of my inability to follow all but a very few conversations, eventually led to

My mother instilled in me a love for reading, which helped me pick up as much information as a child possibly could through the printed word.

my decision to seek employment at Gallaudet College in 1972 after graduation from Washington College, a small liberal arts college on the Eastern Shore of Maryland. I was weary of being alone in the mainstream and eagerly availed myself of the many and varied opportunities offered by what I came to know as the Deaf community.[2]

In 1977, I took a job in the office of Dr. Edward C. Merrill, Jr., then president of Gallaudet. One day, my supervisor gave me a copy of the *Federal Register* and said, "Read through that and highlight anything you think Dr. Merrill should be aware of." My eyes grew wider and wider as I read about the recently enacted Public Law 94–142—the Education for All Handicapped Children Act (now known as the Individuals with Disabilities Education Act—IDEA). I immediately sensed that this law would mean that "all" deaf and hard of hearing children soon would be educated in public schools rather than in the residential schools that the majority of them then attended. My heart sank with despair. "Oh no. . . . Those poor kids will have to go through what I went through."

MOST people have little knowledge of deaf and hard of hearing children and the issues they face. Nor do they know about the Deaf community and the endless array of opportunities it offers regionally, nationally, and internationally. I have come to believe that every adult who has a deaf or hard of hearing child in their circle should know of this community and its history. One cannot understand the issues surrounding these children otherwise.

Deaf and hard of hearing persons today face many of the same struggles faced by their predecessors of past centuries. In recent years, some have suggested that these struggles have not been a result of deafness per se, but rather of educators' and policymakers' decisions about how to deal with deaf and hard of hearing children. The viewpoints of d/Deaf adults themselves, who used to be those children, have infrequently reached the masses. And thus, many solitary children even today may think they are the first and only child to have such struggles.

The more adults become familiar with this common and historical struggle, the more they will be able to impart to their children, deaf *or* hearing, the knowledge and attitudes that will help to minimize these struggles. For my part, I continue this introduction with an encapsulated history of deaf education. I have gleaned what I think are the bare minimum of facts germane to understanding the issues faced by deaf or hard of hearing children who are "included" in the local public school. I am indebted in particular to three scholars: Harlan Lane, Richard Winefield, and Margret Winzer, all of whom have compiled excellent texts on the history of the Deaf community, deaf education, and special education. Their books offer different and complementary information about how educators have viewed and managed d/Deaf people over the past 400 years. Other books add to this overall picture, and I have included a suggested reading list in hopes that readers will be spurred on to learn more.

History directs how most people today think about d/Deaf individuals, and that, in turn, directs how teachers and classmates think about the young deaf and hard of hearing solitaires currently in their midst.[3] Therefore, my goal is to impart three important facts: that the history of deaf education has been fraught with controversy over ideology, that it is only recently that d/Deaf adults themselves have begun to be heard, and that deaf and hard of hearing children bear the consequences of these first two facts.

Evolution of a Controversy

The enduring debate in deaf education has been over the best way to educate and communicate with d/Deaf people. This debate centers around two ideologies—the use of sign language (manualism) and the exclusive use of speech and lipreading (oralism). During the Middle Ages, people with physical impairments as well as those with mental impairments were viewed with scorn, fear, hatred, and pity. They generally had no education, no occupation, and no income. In the sixteenth century, circumstances for d/Deaf individuals began to change when Spain's royal families employed a Benedictine monk, Pedro Ponce de León (1520–1584), to educate their hereditarily deaf members. Ponce recognized that by taking advantage of the deaf boys' intact vision, he could teach them language and, consequently, all other subjects. This is one of the earliest recorded examples of the use of manual, rather than spoken, language as a viable option for deaf children and adults.

A Swiss physician, John Conrad Amman (1669–1724), believed that speech (actually, the voice) was a gift from God and that without spoken language the intellect could not be developed. In Germany as well, Samuel Heinicke (1727–1790) adopted a staunch commitment to the "no speech = no language = no thought" philosophy. Heinicke refused to record his methods, yet he claimed that they worked miracles, and he vigorously criticized manual methods. Both of these men founded oral education programs for deaf children.

In the late 1700s, another monk, Abbé Charles Michel de l'Epée, founded the precursor of the current Institution Nationale des Sourds in Paris. He published two books that explicitly detailed his teaching methodologies—which included ample use of a signed language. When oralist Desire Ordinaire was appointed headmaster of this school in 1822, Deaf alumni took actions that marked the beginning of what is today called the "Deaf community." They left detailed documents and records of their elaborate banquets and other activities, which only in the past few decades have come to light.[4] They thought of Epée as "our spiritual father, our intellectual father, our messiah, our savior, our redeemer." They affirmed that through his efforts, they had gone from "chaos and ignorance" to a viable and happy existence.[5]

In spite of evidence that manual methods resulted in Deaf adults who could command two languages (the signed language and the native written language), teach, and hold other professions, oralism prevailed in other European countries. It became the method of choice in Great Britain as well as in Germany. Thomas Braidwood (1715–1806) and his sons catered to wealthy British parents who paid enormous sums in hopes that their deaf youngsters would be able to participate in the elite social circles. The Braidwoods would only train teachers who were willing to commit to several years of daily constant contact with pupils. Trainees were required to swear that they would not divulge the pedagogical secrets to anyone for a period of seven years. These entrepreneurial leanings contributed in an ironic way to the beginnings of deaf education in the New World.[6]

Thomas Hopkins Gallaudet (1788–1851) and Mason Fitch Cogswell (1761–1830) were neighbors in Hartford, Connecticut. Cogswell had a daughter, Alice, who had become deaf at age four; he and some other parents of deaf children wanted to educate their children. They commissioned Gallaudet to go to Europe to learn how to teach deaf children. Thanks to the inhospitality of the Braidwood family, he went to the Paris school and spent months observing lessons and learning sign language from the Deaf teachers.

In June of 1816, Gallaudet returned to America accompanied by Laurent Clerc, a Deaf teacher from the Paris school. Together, they founded the Connecticut Asylum for the Education and Instruction of Deaf and Dumb Persons in April 1817 (this school, still in operation, is now known as the American School for the Deaf). By 1880, fifty-four similar institutions had been established in other states, and almost all of them endorsed the manual method. These schools employed deaf as well as hearing teachers.

The "war of methods" escalated in 1880 at an international meeting of teachers and administrators from schools for the deaf. This meeting in Milan, Italy, was organized and orchestrated by European oralists who voted that all deaf persons should be taught by the oral method alone because speech "restores the deaf-mute to society" and "places the deaf on the same platform that [hearing persons] occupy."[7]

Shortly thereafter, Deaf adults convened in Cincinnati, Ohio, at the first National Convention of Deaf Mutes. They perceived the decision to ban sign language as insulting, stifling, and ignorant. In the ensuing decades, the Milan decision would remain etched in the minds and hearts of Deaf people—many would decry it as cruel as well as presumptuous.

> 1880 was the year that saw the birth of the infamous Milan resolution that paved the way for foisting upon the deaf everywhere a loathed method; hypocritical in its claims, unnatural in its application, mind-deadening and soul-killing in its ultimate results.[8]

The Milan resolution resulted in a slow but sure decrease in the use of sign language at schools for deaf children and an increase in oral programs all over the world, including the United States. Day schools were founded,

Milan, Italy, 1880 by Mary J. Thornley. Mary was born in Indiana in 1950. She was educated as a solitaire and worked in a factory for ten years. She received an MFA at the University of Washington in 1988. Mary met other Deaf adults when she was in her thirties. Learning about the oral-manual controversy and particularly the Milan conference was eye opening for her. "I realized I was an 'oral experiment,' that I had been told that I was 'treated like everyone else' but that was not true, not even remotely." Her immediate sense of connection to Deaf people is a testament to the bond that is felt when solitaires learn, even in adulthood, of each other's common struggles.

many with strictly oral philosophies, and they hired only hearing teachers. Although these schools officially prohibited sign language, evidence exists that the children nevertheless risked severe punishment by attempting to use sign language whenever possible. Sign language thrived in interactions among students and could not be eradicated. Those who knew, used, and loved sign language refused to abandon it.

In 1890, the arguments among oralists and manualists reached new heights when Edward Miner Gallaudet, son of Thomas Hopkins Gallaudet and president of the National Deaf-Mute College in Washington, D.C., asked Congress for funds to establish a "Normal Department" (to train teachers of the deaf) within the federally supported college. Congress granted the funds against the wishes of the most outspoken oralist of the time—Alexander Graham Bell. While most people know Bell as the inventor of the telephone, few know that he was actually attempting to invent a device to help his deaf wife. In his testimony before Congress, he included the following statements:

> The graduates of the collegiate department are of course deaf. This, therefore, is a proposition to teach deaf persons to teach the deaf. I consider this a backward step, and not a step in advance. Instructors of the deaf, so far as possible, should be in full possession of all their faculties. . . . The employment of deaf teachers is absolutely detrimental to oral instruction, and the training school proposed by President Gallaudet should therefore not be supported by the United States.[9]

Both Alexander Graham Bell and Edward Miner Gallaudet were born to mothers who had hearing impairments. Eliza Bell had been deafened after she acquired speech; she was able to carry on conversations with the aid of an "ear trumpet" (suggesting a relatively mild hearing loss). Sophia Gallaudet was born deaf and for all practical purposes had no usable hearing. Although she could not speak, she could communicate quite well through sign language. Eliza Bell had no interest in associating with other deaf people, except for her daughter-in-law, Mabel Hubbard Bell. Sophia Gallaudet, on the other hand, had attended the American School for four years and served as matron of the National Deaf-Mute College. She lived most of her adult life among other deaf persons.

Bell and Gallaudet engaged in impassioned debate about how people such as their mothers should be educated and, in fact, how they should live. Their contrasting positions provide a backdrop for understanding why we have solitary mainstreamed children today.

A man of many interests and wide influence, Alexander Graham Bell espoused Social Darwinism and a related movement known as eugenics.

The supporters of the eugenics movement believed that the human race could be improved by what was called "purposeful breeding." Bell's contribution to this philosophy appeared in "Memoir Upon the Formation of a Deaf Variety of the Human Race" in 1884. In this paper, he reported his findings that 80 percent of deaf individuals who grew up in institutions (i.e., the deaf schools begun by T. H. Gallaudet and Clerc) married other deaf persons and thus were producing more deaf children. He offered a solution—that congenitally deaf persons be prevented from marrying each other. To that end, he recommended "an end to the segregation of deaf students in special schools, an end to the employment of deaf teachers for deaf students, and an end to the use of sign language."[10]

Edward Miner Gallaudet was more concerned with what was best for the individual deaf person. He observed that teaching deaf children to speak and lipread required extraordinary amounts of time. He felt that this time would be better spent on other learning goals. Since evidence showed that deaf individuals acquired sign language quickly and naturally, academic subjects, character development, and religion could be the real substance of education.

> Under the Manual Method, with oral teaching entirely omitted, the intellectual, moral, and religious training of the whole body of the deaf can be effected much more completely than under the Oral Method . . . . The lack of speech is an inconvenience, but by no means an insuperable barrier to success in business or the attainment of happiness.[11]

The Controversy in Modern Times

From the late nineteenth century until the 1960s, oralism was the dominant method in deaf education. Changes in parental attitudes toward their disabled children led to federal legislation that ultimately has had a tremendous impact on how deaf children are educated. In 1975, President Gerald Ford signed into law the Education for All Handicapped Children Act, also known as Public Law 94–142, which extended equal educational opportunity beyond racial lines to all children with disabilities. Thus, *mainstreaming*—the practice of educating all exceptional children in public schools alongside their "normal" peers—became a household term. The law has been amended twice (once in 1990 and again in 1997) and renamed the Individuals with Disabilities Education Act (IDEA). Its purpose remains the same: "To ensure that all children with disabilities have available to them a free appropriate public education that emphasizes special education and related services designed to meet their unique needs and prepare them for employment and independent living."[12]

In addition to a "free and appropriate public education," IDEA also mandates that each public agency shall ensure (1) that to the maximum extent appropriate, children with disabilities, including children in public or private institutions or other care facilities, are educated with children who are nondisabled; and (2) that special classes, separate schooling or other removal of children with disabilities from the regular educational environment occurs only if the nature or severity of the disability is such that education in regular classes with the use of supplementary aids and services cannot be achieved satisfactorily.[13]

In the mid-1980s, the Regular Education Initiative (REI) pushed the mainstreaming concept even further by advocating that *all* disabled children, both deaf and hard of hearing, be educated in their neighborhood public school as a simple matter of policy. With full inclusion, there is no need for a separate special education system; in a socially just system, the regular classroom teacher must be the teacher for *all* children.[14]

The REI has translated into a slow but steady growth in the number of solitary deaf and hard of hearing children in public schools. The best estimate of the growing number of solitaries is provided every year by the Gallaudet Research Institute, which has conducted and published an *Annual Survey of Deaf and Hard of Hearing Children and Youth* since 1971. In the 1989–1990 school year, there were 4,856 reported solitaires in the United States. By the 2001–2002 school year, this number had grown to 6,379. This recent number represents approximately 15 percent of all *reported* children. In 2001–2002 also, 10,965 children were reported to be in schools with five or less deaf and hard of hearing children. With this figure, fully 40 percent of all U.S. deaf and hard of hearing children have few, if any, same-age peers who are also deaf or hard of hearing.[15] Thus, almost half of all deaf and hard of hearing children are isolated from other deaf and hard of hearing children. A obvious consequence is that the historic deaf schools face shrinking enrollments, and more than several have closed.

It seems that it is all as Dr. Bell intended.

Many educators, parents, and Deaf adults do not believe that the local public school is the least-restrictive environment for many deaf and hard of hearing children. These people began advocating through books, articles, protests, and individual efforts when these laws were first passed. Their hard work continues today to ensure that educational options for deaf and hard of hearing children remain available. Parents who believe their children would be better served in special schools have had to fight for this placement—and this fight can take years, as well as blood, sweat, dollars, and tears. Many grow weary of the fight and must withdraw for the emotional and financial strain it places on the family, and meanwhile the solitaires remain solitaires regardless of whether the placement is good for them or not.

I cannot in the space of this book report on all of the research that supports the idea that deaf and hard of hearing children need each other. Virtually every book and article I read suggests this conclusion. I can, however, provide an inkling of what concerned readers will find if they choose to delve into the suggested reading list.

Claire Ramsey's *Deaf Children in Public Schools* strikes me as unique within the existing literature on deafness, not only for her findings but for her methodology as well.[16] Over the course of a year, she observed the progress of three second-grade deaf students. Because she is both hearing and fluent in sign language, she was privy to what everyone was saying about the three seven-year-old deaf and hard of hearing boys mainstreamed in a local elementary school. And, she was privy to what the boys were saying to each other.

Ramsey's study reveals three important facts. First, she concluded that the school professionals saw themselves *as required by law* to provide inclusion, regardless of whether this setting was best for those boys. Second, she noted that adults would comment frequently that inclusion was good *for the hearing children*, but rarely if ever that it was good for the deaf children. Finally, she observed specific kinds of interaction between the hearing and the deaf children. Almost invariably, the hearing children spoke to the deaf children using directives. And teachers were clueless as to the nature of this interaction.

> The children were doing seatwork and [the teachers] were roaming around the room. Janna [hearing] poked Paul [deaf] and showed him a ring she was wearing. Although Mrs. Rogers did not see Janna get Paul's attention, she did notice that Paul suspended work on his math paper to admire Janna's ring. She called out "Janna please touch Paul." (This was a method she had developed for enlisting the hearing children's help in physically managing the deaf children's attention.) Janna then poked Paul and brusquely signed "Pay Attention," a much more explicit directive than Mrs. Rogers' tone of voice indicated. (70)

Ramsey summarizes her observation in no uncertain terms.

> For the purposes of learning and development, the interaction among deaf and hearing children in the mainstreaming classroom . . . was highly constrained and not developmentally helpful. . . . [The teacher] was correct, however, when she commented that the deaf and hearing children did not appear to be mean or rude to each other. . . . However, few parents of hearing children would judge sufficient for their own children the personal contact and peer interaction that was available in the mainstream for deaf second graders at Aspen School (fictitious name). (74)

The oral-manual controversy continues as growing numbers of educated deaf persons and their hearing supporters publish their research and memoirs, revamp special schools, establish charter schools, and fill the staffing needs of a proliferation of university-level American Sign Language and Deaf Studies programs. Much of their work promotes education for deaf children in schools/programs that are couched in the philosophies of bilingualism. A common thread is the cry for the recognition of sign languages as viable, practical, and even excellent.

> The mistaken belief that [American Sign Language] is a set of simple gestures with no internal structure has led to the tragic misconception that the relationship between Deaf people to their sign language is a casual one that can be easily severed and replaced. This misconception more than any other has driven educational policy. Generations of school children have been

forbidden to use signs and compelled to speak. Other children have been urged to use artificially modified signs in place of vocabulary from the natural sign language.[17]

The works by Deaf scholars have further declared that the Regular Education Initiative is *not* in the best interests of deaf and hard of hearing children and, in fact, can be detrimental to their emotional as well as their academic well-being.[18] As Winzer summarizes in her history of special education:

> Mainstreaming remains an unproven educational panacea; there seems to be no true answer as to whether regular class settings are superior for exceptional students. Most of the zeal for the practice has stemmed from its anticipated effects in the social and emotional domain, which includes removal of the stigma associated with special education classes, enhancement of the status of handicapped youngsters with their nonhandicapped peers, [and] promotion of learning through modeling of appropriate behavior by nonhandicapped students.[19]

Author's Note

Children of My Heart was the first title I envisioned for this book. In just four words, this phrase describes the depth of feeling I have for all deaf and hard of hearing children. Living with my father, who also had a hearing loss, intimately connected me with the controversies surrounding sign language, deaf history, and deaf children. Our lives were and are inextricably tied, and it is curious how we chose such different ways of dealing with our hearing loss. My father remained in the hearing world his entire life. He laughed when others laughed and smirked when others smirked. Not only that, but I feel certain he knew of the Deaf community, because he worked for almost thirty years at the *New York Daily News,* and I know from my conversations with other Deaf people that many Deaf men worked there during the 1950s, 1960s, and 1970s. Yet, my father never once mentioned this to me.

I saw the impact of his struggles (and my struggles) on my mother, my siblings, their children, and even our extended family. My heart aches for relationships that were marred by a lack of knowledge and understanding. My heart aches for never having known my hard of hearing grandfather and great-grandmother. But most of all, my heart aches for deaf children today, especially those who are solitaires in hearing schools.

On one of those few occasions where my father and I did discuss hearing loss, he suggested that I "do something to help people who cannot hear." When he died on my forty-sixth birthday, the drive to produce this book began to grow from embers to fire. I began to feel compelled to produce a work that would illuminate the issues over which he and I had so passionately disagreed. I could not understand how we could differ so much in our perspectives concerning our shared uniqueness. I felt that he denied himself and our family so much joy by refusing to learn sign language. His recalcitrance greatly saddened me. I wanted my work to shed light on our opposing ideas about deafness. Frankly, I wanted to produce a work that would help others avoid what I perceived as the pitfalls my father stumbled into and from which he never escaped.

I reached out to adults who were also mainstreamed as solitaires for all or most of their K–12 years. I invited them to correspond with me electronically about their experiences, a task that they gladly accepted. They concurred that the labels, solitary and solitaire, encapsulated their experiences. I collected and analyzed their writings, shared my analyses with them, and included many of their comments in this book.

Over the years, I have met people who would put me on a pedestal, declaring that I was somehow unique, better, different than "those other deaf people." In their effort to lift me up, they put others down, albeit unintentionally. I want very much to make the point that my story is *not* unique. Every solitaire made their own unique points. I am deeply grateful for their willingness to share their stories, enthusiasm, and love for deaf and hard of hearing children with me, and with you.

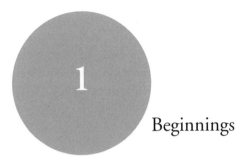

Beginnings

Like most of the kids who lived on my small town street circa 1955, I was destined to attend Cos Cob School, which was just up the street from our house on Mead Avenue. It was probably the third week of my kindergarten career, and Miss Voight's class was having a regular Monday morning. Our days always started with some playtime. We would play with the big blocks, the child-sized log cabin, and other toys as everyone arrived, hung up their jackets, and put their freshly washed naptime blankets in their cubbyholes. At some point, Miss Voight would start to plunk out a little tune on her piano.

By now, all the children knew that this little tune was a call to put down their toys and come sit near the piano. "Come and sit down, come and sit down, come and sit down right now," she would play and sing. Once they were assembled around the piano, Miss Voight greeted the children, and told them they were going to play a new game.

They would sit in a circle in the middle of the room, on the floor. They would close their eyes and sit quietly. When the piano music started again, they were to open their eyes, stand up, and begin walking in the circle that they had been sitting in. So over to the middle of the room they went, as Miss Voight instructed them to sit on the floor in a circle, cross-legged. "All right now everyone close your eyes, and when you hear the music, stand up and begin to walk in a circle this way (she gestured clockwise)." The twenty four- and five-year-olds did as they were told and patiently waited for the music to begin.

One little girl waited very patiently indeed. She waited and waited. Her eyes were closed; her chin was on her little fists, her elbows on her knees. She waited. And waited. It seemed like an awfully long time. She wondered if she should peek. She wondered for a minute or so. Finally she decided to peek. Much to her dismay, every child was standing up and walking in a circle! Only she was still seated, waiting for the music to start. She looked over to the piano and saw Miss Voight playing it. The embarrassment that the little girl felt was deep and lasting.

That little girl was me. This was the first time I realized there was something different about me. I don't remember thinking "I didn't hear the music." I just remember feeling embarrassed.

From the time I entered school, I had a serious problem. The worst part was that I was the only child in school with such a problem, and the adults around me did not know how to help me. No one knew what to do to help this solitary young girl, the only one in the school with a hearing loss. This quandary plagued me until I took matters into my own hands at age twenty.

Like Father, Like Daughter?

I grew up in New England, the middle of five widely spaced children, to parents who were both from immigrant families. My mother knew my father had a hearing loss when she married him, as did his father, grandmother, and one of his uncles. They all functioned just like ordinary people. So when Miss Voight called her to express concern about me, my mother was not surprised. She promptly took me to the Greenwich Hospital Speech and Hearing Clinic, and soon I had my first hearing aid at age five. The audiologist surmised that the loss had been gradual because my language development was normal and I was already (the tests showed) an expert lipreader.

From then on, my mother would remind me, "Gina, you have to tell people that you can't hear them." But at a very young age, I came to dread telling other people. As an adult, I recognized, on my own, a very important reason for this dread. Telling them did not solve the problem. Telling

I was the middle child out of five.

them didn't change the fact that I could not hear them. And in reality, it wasn't that I couldn't "hear" them.

During my elementary years, I had a 50-dB hearing loss. I could hear people's voices, but my speech discrimination was such that unless we were in a quiet environment *and* by a stroke of luck or the grace of God they spoke clearly, everything sounded like a bunch of noisy gibberish. The kids at Cos Cob School and on Mead Avenue, with very rare exception, didn't know what to do in order for me to be able to decipher their cacophony. Even the adults didn't know.

Gradually, I learned that certain remedial actions helped somewhat, but only in some situations. If I was with just one other child, the environment and the other child's way of talking (loudness, lip movements, etc.) could be controlled to my benefit. In the public school classrooms of the 1950s and 1960s, there was enough peace and quiet that at least through elementary school I could hear and lipread my teachers. But I couldn't hear and lipread when two or more other kids were talking the way kids talk—animated and often simultaneously. Ever. No amount of explanation or pleading or demonstrating would make it possible for me to be privy to the chattering for more than a few minutes. The kind of support I needed went against everyday ways of conversation.

As an adult, I found out that there were many other children who "can't hear too well" and who grew up as the only such child in their school. I learned that I wasn't, after all, the only one who had this experience, which I came to call "the solitary mainstream experience." I learned that over the centuries, during my own growing-up years and still today, such children have been in schools all over the United States, and, indeed, the world. I surmised that they might be like me—not knowing who to tell or how to tell or what to do about it. Later on, I surmised that other adults like me, who had been through this experience, would be very happy to share their tales so that the children of today might have an easier time of it.

The Importance of Making a Contribution

It is a rather funny story how I first attempted to compensate for the deficiency I became aware of in that kindergarten classroom. As the kid who "couldn't hear too well," it was important to my self-esteem that I could contribute to my world (though I only know this in retrospect). My contribution was to invent a recreational activity for the neighborhood children: Coke bottle fishing.

The supplies used were real glass Coke bottles (one for each fisherperson), some durable string (the kind we used was white, soft, and absorbent), and whatever amount of white bread a mother could spare. On many a summer morning, we would haul our supplies over to the local mill pond that was quite close to our homes. There was plenty of edge access, and plenty of minnows, or as we called them "killies." We had several "good spots" where the fishing was terrific.

Here is the technique: First, we tied the string around the mouth of the bottle. Then we made it fit snugly in the little furrow that was just below the bottle top, so it wouldn't slip off. Then, we broke up the bread and stuffed it inside the bottle. We then walked down to the shore and carefully dipped our bottles in the water, so that the water seeped in. When our bottle was more than half full of water, we threw it out into the water about five feet from the shore. Assuming the pond water was reasonably clear (and it was in those days), we would be able to see the bread inside the bottle. Assuming also there are ample minnows, in just a minute or two, we would notice the bread being jerked erratically as it was torn to pieces by voracious little mouths. Then we scooped up the bottle, and the bounty was ours. Most of these "killies" were about two inches long, but sometimes we would catch what we called "big fat ones" that were almost four inches long.

What did we do with our catch? For a while, we would just collect them in a bucket of water until our glee for the activity was satiated. Then we would mercifully toss them back. At one point, however, I had a slightly fiendish idea. My cat! I must have just read a book or seen a cartoon about cats eating fish and was intrigued to see if real live cats would eat real live fish. For some time thereafter, my cat probably thought he had died and gone to cat heaven. Then, alas, my mother put a stop to this foolishness. I wonder if she issued the cease and desist order for the sake of the "killies" or the cat.

From my conversations with other deaf and hard of hearing adults,[1] I now realize that when we were in the early elementary years, communication was fairly simple, and it was easy for us to become leaders of activities such as Coke bottle fishing. We may also have been good in sports and were picked first for teams. But as we got older and moved from the local elementary school to the local middle school and high school, interactions became increasingly problematic. Then, it became really difficult to make a contribution in either activities or conversations.

Finding "My People"

Hearing loss made me different from the other students during all of my K–12 years. This difference colored, overshadowed, permeated, and consumed every single school day of my life. It was always just "there" and it threatened to become a lifelong state of affairs. Little did I know that things were about to change dramatically as I sat in the Washington College cafeteria in Chestertown, Md., during the fall semester of my freshman year. We were having lunch, me and my fellow freshman acquaintances.

They chattered endlessly about God knows what. I never knew what people were talking about at mealtimes. Or at parties. Or at football games. That was life as I knew it, and there just wasn't anything anyone could do about it. I looked like everyone else but felt like I was surrounded by an invisible glass wall that made all voices sound garbled.

Like my father, I had learned to copy interacting behaviors, laughing when the other kids laughed, and smirking when they smirked. I had also learned that if I asked anyone to repeat anything, they would say "I'll tell you later" or "It's not important." I could discern their voices with my hearing aid, but because of the nature of severe hearing loss, the only time I could successfully use my lipreading skills to fill in the gaps was if only one person was talking in a very quiet environment and that person enunciated his or her words clearly and distinctly, as my kindergarten teacher had.

Because of this inability to follow conversations, my habit was to busy myself with my lunch while the other girls blabbed away. But on that day, I happened to look up, and over on the other side of the cafeteria I noticed a group of young men engaged in the most animated conversation I had ever seen in my life. My eyes fixed on them. My heart felt this intense grasping or longing like I had never felt before. I felt incredibly drawn to them and thought, "Oh! My people!"

These young men were having their animated conversation in American Sign Language (ASL), although I didn't know this at the time. I soon learned that they were deaf and that they were the members of the Gallaudet College soccer team. To this day, I marvel at the depth of feeling that I had for this group of strangers. I had never seen anyone signing ASL before. And yet, I knew instinctively that I had an indelible bond with them. They were like me. I was like them.

Taking Matters into My Own Hands

I knew I had to find a way to join my people. So, in my junior year, I arranged to spend my senior year at Gallaudet. That decision to enter the Deaf world, made at the age of twenty, was the best decision I have ever made in my life.

Over the next few decades, I learned a new way of living. I learned that by using sign language, I could participate in group discussions. During my

The entire Oliva clan at Mom's eightieth birthday party. We have had four more great-grandkids since then!

K–12 years, everyone thought I was very shy. I learned later that I wasn't shy at all—just deaf! I could be a committee chairperson, a teacher, or a group exercise instructor. Within the Deaf world, my life became full, vibrant, satisfying; I could function at my full potential. Gallaudet and my new friends became a home away from home—a real home where I could be myself, and be everything I was capable of. No longer was I trapped in a world where I could not be myself.

As mentioned earlier, my father grew up as a solitaire and he chose to remain as the only deaf or hard of hearing person in his circle for his entire adult life. I, on the other hand, made a decision to immerse myself in the Deaf community. I spent a good part of my twenties trying to convince my family to learn sign language. Dad had no interest. "I'm too old to learn," he would say. He was about fifty at the time, the same age I am as I write this book.

During my adult years, Dad and I had just a few exchanges that starkly illustrated our polar opposition regarding how deaf people should be and

what they could be. Our opposing views echoed, in my view, the controversy that has marred progress in the field of deaf education since the sixteenth century. His view was clear in one conversation that happened in
March of 1988. As chance would have it my parents were visiting at my
home in Maryland during the now-famous Deaf President Now protest at
Gallaudet.[2] My father remarked, "Well, I think the college ought to have a
president who can hear. A deaf person could not do that job." I decided to
take the easiest way out and replied, "Let's not talk about this." My father
and I only had one terrible argument about hearing loss—and once was
enough (the story is related in chapter 4). My mother wisely said nothing
as well, but I am sure she would have disagreed with Dad.

Contrasting Viewpoints

Sometimes how one group labels a certain phenomenon is different from
how another group labels the same phenomenon. Rhetorical analysis
delves into such contrasts. For instance, the European conquest of America, from the European perspective, was a necessity to progress. The subsequent impact on the Indian nation, from the perspective of the Native
Americans, was hardly progress. Likewise, the forceful taking of Africans
from their homeland for enslaved farm work was upright business for
some and deplorably immoral for others.

Another example of such contrasting labeling, *albeit not within a category of outright and forceful physical domination,* is the solitary mainstream
experience. I pondered long and hard about how to label this phenomenon.
Those three words, for me, come as close as any to accurately labeling this
experience. Other deaf and hard of hearing adults who offered their
thoughts for this book never questioned the label. Former solitaires knew
instinctively that this was an appropriate label.

In contrast, experts in the field of special education use the term *inclusion* to describe the practice of placing a single deaf or hard of hearing child
(or any disabled child, actually) within a local school. Certainly *inclusion*
has very different connotations than "the solitary mainstream" or "alone in
the mainstream." It is a very different kind of label indeed for the phenomenon in question.

What does that word *inclusion* bring to mind? That's simple—it means to be included: certainly a normal, to-be-expected state of affairs. The word seems to go hand in hand with another catchall term used today: *diversity.* America has embraced diversity as a value—that although we are all unique, we need to accept and respect our differences. There is no reason for special schools or clubs or programs for certain categories of people. Most adults, even adults who have no involvement in education, human services, or politics, would probably say, "That sounds good. Of course, everyone should be included—so this inclusion philosophy must be a wonderful thing."

It is my premise that true inclusion for individual deaf children is a possibly unreachable ideal. My experience with inclusion in the public school system from 1955 to 1968 was far from ideal. To me, my experience was solitary. I was alone. I was not included. And this is not because I was educated a long time ago. It is because real inclusion for a deaf or hard of hearing child was and continues to be extremely difficult to achieve. The adults in the schools and neighborhoods where solitaires live don't know how to achieve it. Without ample and extraordinary help and support, for a neighborhood school or local education system to develop the conditions by which a single deaf or hard of hearing child would be truly included in all of her or his K–12 classrooms could take so long that the child will have grown up and graduated before it happened. Further, whether or not ample help and support *could* result in a truly inclusive experience for a solitary deaf or hard of hearing child is still an open question today. Many Deaf (and hearing) adults are skeptical about this possibility.

> Public schools are not likely to understand the need for a community of Deaf people; public schools with mainstreamed deaf children are often only minimally connected to the surrounding community of Deaf people. The result of these changes [towards more mainstreaming of deaf children] is that there are many young deaf children who . . . have never met a Deaf person and have never seen American Sign Language. . . . The new social order of "mainstreaming," instead of introducing new worlds to deaf children, may well lead them to a new kind of isolation.[3]

My investigation of recent scholarly works suggests that the policy of inclusion has yet to result in better educational experiences, on a broad scale, for deaf and hard of hearing children. Yet ideals are meant to be pursued. How can we hasten environmental and social conditions that do allow effective inclusion for deaf and hard of hearing children and adults? And, what resources or methods should we use to find the answer to this question?

Finding the Answers

How should we answer such questions? How can we effect positive change for each solitaire, and for his parents and teachers? Those parents and teachers may also feel alone in this task. For many of them, this deaf child may be the first deaf person they have ever met.

And perhaps therein lies the crux of the matter. Deaf people have for too long been in the closets, the back rooms, out of sight and out of mind. For this reason, I embarked on an effort to include a large number of other adults who had been solitaires in my effort to provide information to parents and other people concerned with the young solitaires of today. It is my hope that this book will inform readers of a perspective that must always be sought by schools, parents, neighbors, and classmates when a deaf or hard of hearing child is "included" in their midst: the perspective of deaf and hard of hearing adults.

> I believe that an adult's reflection of his or her K–12 years as the only deaf student is crucially the most powerful "voice" in studying and understanding "the solitary mainstream experience" of deaf individuals. They, like myself, are truly the ones that went through the experience and need to be allowed to speak of their experience. They must be involved with the parents' decision on how to meet their deaf children's social and academic needs in a K–12 setting. M 89[4]

> As a deaf person who grew up with limited contact to other deaf people, but who was very successfully mainstreamed, I feel like I have great insight into the problems faced by solitary mainstreamed students, as well as into ways to deal with those problems. I think I can provide encouragement for those who are in similar situations right now. Maybe they will shed fewer tears than I did if they know more about what to expect and how to approach various issues. F 93

2

Lessons from the Neighborhood

BEFORE I dive into what the Solitary Mainstream Project participants had to say in retrospect, I would first like to share some explorations and ruminations about our world—the world in which we found ourselves in the last half of the twentieth century. When I speak of "our world," I am referring not so much to a world devoid of sound, or a world with sound that sounds funny. Rather I am referring to the world of people surrounding us, people who have beliefs and attitudes about children and adults who are deaf or hard of hearing. A world where all children receive messages about their own position and status in the larger world, deaf and hard of hearing children being no exception. To most readers, this world is just *the world*. It's round, and has countries, trees, flowers, cars, buildings, and people. Most readers, unless they are deaf or hard of hearing, will have a hard time imagining a world that looks, sounds, and feels different. From one perspective, I lived in the same world that my hearing siblings did. But that world looked, sounded, and felt different to me. I would challenge the non-deaf reader to *try* to view this world as it looks, sounds, and feels to the deaf or hard of hearing child, in order to understand how this world becomes a lonely place in which to be. The world of the deaf or hard of hearing child also has countries, trees, flowers, cars, and buildings. But the people, to us, are perplexing. They move their mouths a lot. That's called "talking." They do this "talking" all the time unless they are asleep. This talking involves making sound, but the sound that comes out, if we hear it, just sounds like gibberish. The more we grow and the more we become aware that this "talking" is what binds people together, the more we feel left out—we are not a part of that world. We can be systematically taught what these sounds mean—but spoken language doesn't become infused in us like it does in our hearing siblings and peers. It's not because our brains are defective, it's because our hearing mechanism is defective. We can nevertheless become fluent in a spoken or written language with patient and loving teaching. But we will probably always feel, in some or many situations, that we are not fully a part of that "talking world."

Ways of thinking about deaf and hard of hearing people can come from actual encounters, from media portrayals, from what you overhear your mother saying about some kid, or from a variety of indirect information sources. I think it is valuable to explore what we learn about d/Deaf people, through little effort of our own, in our very own neighborhoods.

During my senior year of college, and my first year at Gallaudet, my childhood friend, Mary Ellen, was considering moving to D.C. and thus came to visit me. We were both twenty years old. We had grown up across the street from each other, sharing kickball games, chats about boys, lots of high school dances, and many other experiences. I will never forget that after a short time on campus, she looked at me very solemnly and said, "Gina, you don't belong here."

My childhood friend didn't think of me as deaf. To her mind, d/Deaf people like those she saw around her at Gallaudet, and me, Gina, were *not* alike. For some reason, she thought of me as different from them, somehow better than them. I feel fairly certain that she had never read a book about d/Deaf people, had never met a d/Deaf person other than me, and had not learned about d/Deaf people in school. Yet, she had some very firm ideas about the students she saw around Gallaudet. What were these ideas she had? What had influenced her thinking? Why did she think of d/Deaf people as so lacking? Obviously she did not learn about d/Deaf people from history books or the Internet. And there were no d/Deaf people on television at that time.

Lessons from Elementary School Classrooms in the Late Twentieth Century

While we don't have research to tell us how my contemporaries (such as Mary Ellen) viewed deaf and hard of hearing children, we do have research from more recent years. This research helps us to see what societal messages hearing children are receiving about their deaf and hard of hearing classmates.

Ramsey witnessed the hearing children using their limited sign language vocabulary to interact with the deaf boys in limited and sometimes demeaning ways. An example of what she labeled "directives and hints" was discussed in the introduction. Ramsey labeled another category of interaction as "evaluations." The hearing children would sometimes sign GOOD, to a deaf classmate even when the deaf classmate was not looking at them. The interactions between her deaf informants and their hearing classmates was limited to instrumental communication, e.g., questions and answers about schoolwork or expectations, with deaf children doing the asking and the hearing children doing the answering.[1] It seems safe to conclude that the hearing children somehow received the message "the way to interact with deaf and hard of hearing people is to tell them what to do."

Michelle Yetman conducted a sociometric study that speaks volumes about how hearing children view their deaf and hard of hearing classmates.[2]

Children's perception of how significant others view them is critical to the development of their self esteem. Scholars have long considered the concept of self to be developed through interactions with others. As a child interacts with adults and with other children, he learns how these adults and children view him, and internalizes the perceptions of others about himself.[3]

Sociometrics explores how children rate their classmates and peers by asking them to respond to statements such as "name three classmates you really like and three classmates you do not." The resulting analysis helps to differentiate four general groups of children: popular children, rejected children, neglected children, and controversial children. Popular children are those who are frequently placed in the "popular" category—many children like them. Rejected children are those who are actively disliked by many children.

Neglected children are like rejected children in that they lack friends but are not actively disliked. Finally, controversial children have some peers who actively like them and some who actively dislike them. It has been found that ratings are relatively stable over time (e.g., children found to be popular or rejected in their early years generally remain so for their entire school careers). Further, various studies have shown that children found to be rejected or neglected are at a higher risk for social and psychiatric problems in adolescence and adulthood.[4] Yetman's study of mainstreamed deaf and hard of hearing children showed that 75 percent of these children were in the neglected category and none were in the popular category.[5]

Using another measure of self esteem, Yetman found that the deaf and hard of hearing children had significantly lower self esteem in three out of

My childhood friend Mary Ellen holds one of Dad's artworks.

five areas: academic competence, social competence, and behavioral conduct.[6] They expressed dissatisfaction with their academic achievements and with their ability to make friends. Her analysis revealed that the more hours per week deaf and hard of hearing children spent in direct contact with hearing children (i.e., the more time deaf and hard of hearing children spent in regular classes as opposed to special education classes), the lower their self esteem score. This finding demonstrates a phenomenon known as the "referent group." Children (and adults) compare themselves to a referent group. The more time a deaf child spent with hearing children, the more likely she was to compare herself to her hearing peers. However, those children who used their deaf and hard of hearing peers as a referent group had higher levels of self esteem.

It seems logical to think that children with less severe hearing losses would be better able to succeed in the regular school environment. After all, they are "just hard of hearing." Yetman's study does not support that supposition—more than half of the students in Yetman's study could be classified as hard of hearing (60 percent had mild to moderately severe hearing losses). The results demonstrated that the children's degree of hearing loss had no significant impact on their sociometric standing or their self esteem. Even children classified as "only" hard of hearing can be rejected by their hearing classmates and thus suffer.

Yetman also administered questionnaires to the teachers of forty-one deaf students. She found that teachers consistently rated deaf and hard of hearing students as less competent than the hearing students in all tested areas. This is a sad fact considering that she did her study in the last few years of the twentieth century, almost twenty-five years after the passage of P.L. 94–142.

Lessons from Hearing Children Born to Deaf Parents

Families where one or both parents are culturally Deaf have borne hearing children throughout the ages.[7] These hearing children can tell us some important things about how people who can hear have looked at people who cannot. In books and articles by these children, they provide evidence that a negative view of d/Deaf people has been passed down from generation to generation.

The majority of children born to Deaf parents are, in fact, hearing. Many of these children grow up to call themselves CODAs (children of Deaf adults) and actively participate in a growing national organization formed to support the common history and goals of these unique individuals.[8] Perhaps, more than anyone, these individuals understand both worlds: Deaf and hearing.

Not only have CODAs organized themselves and reached out to others like themselves, but they have also written books about their experiences. The following excerpt from Paul Preston's *Mother Father Deaf* demonstrates how hearing children in public schools probably think about their deaf and hard of hearing classmates.

> My grandparents still don't sign. My grandfather's passed away, never knowing how to sign. My grandmother's still alive, and the only way they [my grandmother and my father] communicate is passing notes. And I kind of look down on that, and plus the way she [grandmother] talks to us. My father still doesn't know how she talks to us. She'll say, "It's really amazing how your father's kept a job, and has a house and raised fine kids." And I'm thinking, why are you so shocked? I can't understand why they're so shocked. To me they're just as normal as anybody else. But even their own parents look at them and think it's a big deal if they can drive or walk down the street.[9]

Thus, a family with deaf members frequently has what CODAs call the sandwich phenomena, which occurs when (1) the grandparents can hear; (2) The parents are deaf or hard of hearing; (3) The next generation, the CODA himself, can hear; (4) The CODA learns sign, often as a first language, because his or her parents use ASL as their primary language in the home; and (5) The grandparents never learn to sign. *Mother Father Deaf* and Lou Ann Walker's *A Loss for Words* are just two of several books published in recent years by hearing people who grew up surrounded by deaf and hard of hearing people.

> The deaf relatives would sit in the living room, eating on TV trays. And the hearing relatives would be in the dining room. And every now and then someone from one room would get up and go into the other room and look around and nod and smile. Then they'd come back and sit down. Who knows what they were doing. Maybe they wanted to make sure everybody was still alive.[10]

These hearing children were often asked and expected to serve as go-betweens between their parents and their grandparents. As many CODAs grew up, they learn ways to extract themselves from this role and allow hearing grandparents, as well as other family members, to live with the consequences of their decisions to not learn to sign. In their own way, CODAS who do learn sign find ways to send the message to their non-signing grandparents that they love and accept their Deaf parents, and that they even feel grateful that because of these parents, they know two languages and have been privileged to be part of the Deaf community.

One young CODA woman painfully witnessed the attitudinal difference between her paternal grandparents (who were deaf) and her maternal grandparents (who were hearing) and how the beliefs of the latter caused great pain to the family. When the CODA's mother had become pregnant with her, the maternal grandparents were appalled because they had tried to dissuade their daughter from having children, fearing that, God forbid, the child might be deaf. When the CODA was born and found to be hearing, the maternal grandparents were elated. As the girl grew up, her maternal grandmother would tell her frequently that the grandmother's beautiful diamond wedding ring would someday be hers. It was obvious to this girl, even at a very young age, that the grandmother was skipping a generation in her planned bequeathal. The wedding ring would go directly to the hearing granddaughter, skipping over the Deaf daughter.

When the grandmother died, an uncle handed an envelope containing the precious ring to the young CODA woman. The young woman, however, refused to take part in this discriminating scenario. She said to her uncle, "Please take this ring. Give it to my mother."[11]

These stories profoundly demonstrate the ideas that many contemporary Americans have about deaf individuals within their own families. In the following excerpt, Lou Ann Walker offers further information about how neighbors viewed her Deaf parents, as evidenced by stares or overheard comments that became part of their shared experience.

> I could never bring myself to tell Mom and Dad about the garage mechanic who refused to serve them because they were deaf, or the kids at school who made obscene gestures mocking our sign language. Not once did I convey the questions asked literally hundreds of times: "Does your father have a job?"

"Are they allowed to drive?" Those questions carried an implicit insult to families such as ours, which was proud and hard-working and self-sufficient.[12]

Preston's informants expressed concern that readers would feel that any problems in a family with Deaf parents would be caused *because* the parents were deaf. In other words, they were painfully aware of an apparently pervasive disdain held by others toward their Deaf parents.

> You think I'd tell anyone that there were problems? Can you imagine what they would say? "Oh, it must be because your parents are deaf." It doesn't matter that other families have problems too. What family doesn't have problems? But if my family had problems, then it's all because my parents are deaf.[13]

The hearing children of Deaf parents are privy, on a daily basis, to comments made about d/Deaf people. Hearing people make remarks in the proximity of d/Deaf people assuming no one will hear. Little do they know that the ten-year-old who they think is deaf like her parents is really a hearing sponge who soaks up their comments. What's more, this ten-year-old takes the remarks to heart because she has a natural loyalty and profound understanding of both the strengths and vulnerabilities of her parents.

Many CODAs feel that deafness itself is not a problem—the problem stems from how people who *can* hear view and react to d/Deaf individuals. Preston's informants spent much of their childhood explaining to hearing people about deafness, and they lamented that they would often tire of "explaining about" their experiences as CODAs to people who were clueless about what being a CODA meant or about what deafness meant.

CODAs who reported these incidents came from all over the United States and a few other countries. This is compelling anecdotal evidence that most people know very little about the strengths of d/Deaf people and thus will not have the insight necessary to optimally support the solitary young deaf and hard of hearing children they may find in their midst.

The role of informing the hearing world of the plight of d/Deaf individuals continues for many CODAs into adulthood. A significant number become sign language interpreters. It is generally accepted within the Deaf community that CODA interpreters are often the best interpreters because they are often truly bilingual—fluent in both English and ASL. In addition, they have an understanding of the culture and the nuances or communication between Deaf and hearing people, and they have a naturally acquired skill at facilitating such communication.

Lessons from Sign Language Interpreters

Some of today's solitary mainstreamed children have sign language interpreters in their schools. CODA interpreters who work in educational settings have a unique insight because they have been exposed to many Deaf individuals, have even known them as family members, and are keenly aware that Deaf people are capable of far more than what many teachers might expect from a deaf or hard of hearing child in a public school. The following quote is from a CODA who worked as an interpreter in a public school:

> It's a few minutes before the class will start. Everyone's fishing notebooks from knapsacks and sharpening pencils, and it's all "What did you put for the last answer on the algebra?" and "Tomorrow's the last day for yearbook money, right?" and "If we want to stay for the game, Toni says she can give us a ride." All of the eleventh-graders are speaking or listening, directly or indirectly. Except for one student, sitting down front. She is neither speaking nor listening; she is not involved; she is deaf.
>
> I am her sign language interpreter. I stand at the front of the class, posed to begin signing whenever she looks at me, but she doesn't; she is resting her eyes on the sky outside the window. When at last she does turn her face, it is not to see what her classmates are saying but to chat with me about her weekend, about the book I am reading, about her dog, my sweater, anything. She is hungry for communication and chooses me—an adult satellite paid to follow her through the school day—rather than her peers, who do not speak her language.
>
> Class begins. She pays attention for a while. Sometimes when the teacher asks a question, she signs a response, which I interpret into spoken English—always a little late, just a few seconds after the other students. Sometimes the students will talk at once; their voices overlap and I have to

choose one thread to follow, or compress them all in a quick synopsis, inserting who said which thing to whom and in what tone of voice.[14]

Of utmost importance are the questions: Is an interpreted education an appropriate education? Is it an adequate education? An equal education? Perhaps most importantly, if a parent or teacher could really fathom the world of a child receiving an interpreted education, would that parent or teacher view such an education as satisfactory and acceptable?

Unfortunately, the answers to these questions are still a judgment call, and the call to judgment falls on the parents of deaf children. Parents become quickly aware of the general ignorance of hearing people about the shared experiences and needs of deaf and hard of hearing children and their families. They become aware that they too are alone in their quandry.

Lessons from Parents with Grown Deaf Children

Susan Gregory, Juliet Bishop, and Lesley Sheldon conducted a noteworthy longitudinal study of British deaf and hard of hearing children and their parents. They interviewed the parents when the children were young and then interviewed them again eighteen years later. Upon looking back on their years raising their children, who were now young adults, many parents decried the lack of information they had during their child's school years. This is expressed most poignantly in the words of one mother:

> I could never see the light at the end of the tunnel. I could never see [her deaf daughter] developing into the person she is today. I felt she would be always and forever needing help, which she doesn't. . . . People are not quite sure what to do about her. It's not that they mean to be that way, they just don't know how to go on. The truth of the matter is that there is not enough known about deafness.[15]

Lessons from Those Who Lose Their Hearing in Adulthood

For a final source of evidence of the pervasive ignorance about d/Deaf people among the hearing population, we can explore the writings of people who lose their hearing in adulthood. These are people who suddenly find themselves facing deafness, knowing nothing about it, and being suddenly thrust face to face with previously unfathomable discrimination.

The following excerpt, from R. H. Smith's *The Case about Amy*, describes a late deafened adult's experiences upon losing his hearing.

> It was a jolt to Chatoff to discover his new status and to realize what it meant. In the eyes of others, he was "handicapped," and this meant that people had begun to view him in terms of his disability, rather than his abilities. He found that, for most people, to know that someone was "deaf" was to know all it was necessary to know about that person. He could feel people shrink discreetly away from him. He asked himself if he had held that attitude himself before becoming deaf and he remembered his discomfiture at the deaf people signing in the restaurant.[16]

The term *late deafened* is usually reserved for individuals such as Chatoff, the man referred to in the previous quote.[17] Several other people have written books about their experiences of becoming deaf in their adult years. Often, the first thing that late deafened people become aware of is that hearing people in general have neither patience for nor knowledge of the unique needs of an individual with a hearing loss.

In this chapter, I have tried to illustrate what may be the crux of the issues faced by solitary deaf and hard of hearing children today. According to the hearing children of Deaf parents, according to the hearing parents of deaf and hard of hearing children, and according to hearing people who find themselves suddenly deafened, hearing people generally don't know much about deafness. Further, a noticeable number of hearing people appear to harbor unflattering opinions about this most misunderstood of all human predicaments.

How does this lack of understanding manifest itself in our elementary, middle, and secondary schools? How does it impact peer relationships and specifically how deaf and hard of hearing children are viewed by their hearing peers? How does it affect the lives of solitary mainstreamed deaf and hard of hearing children? Who better to ask than the adults who were once those children?

A Glimpse at Everyday Life

WHEN my mother first read *Deaf in America,* a landmark book about the Deaf community, she objected to a term she came across—*hearing person.*[1] "I don't like being called a *hearing person,*" she said. "I'm just a person!" I explained to her that when I first arrived at Gallaudet and heard the term, I too thought it was weird. But I have come to learn that it was a necessary descriptor for use in conversation about issues related to hearing loss. So I must emphasize that *hearing person* is never used in this book in a derogatory fashion. *Hearing* is simply an adjective used to distinguish between the subjects of this book: the solitary deaf or hard of hearing individuals and the hearing people around them. It is no different than a book about race relations referring to individuals as black or white.

So, what is daily life really like for deaf or hard of hearing children who grow up in a hearing neighborhood and attend the same schools as everyone else? How do hearing adults and children in neighborhood schools, most having never experienced life with a hearing loss, behave toward such a child? What does their behavior suggest about their attitudes toward d/Deaf people?

To explore how society's ideas about d/Deaf people have translated into the attitudes and behavior of teachers and students toward deaf and hard of hearing schoolchildren, I took a sabbatical in the year 2000 and embarked on what I decided to call the Solitary Mainstream Project. All of the participants who volunteered for this study had college educations. Deaf or hard of hearing adults who did *not* do well academically in the mainstream are unlikely to voluntarily participate in research studies. Identifying and locating such adults would be quite difficult. Their voice is sorely lacking and sorely needed.

For interested readers, a description of the methods I used and a summary of participant characteristics are included in the Appendix.

I initially asked participants to tell me anything they wished about their experiences growing up as the only deaf or hard of hearing child in their school. From these writings, I determined four general themes and asked them to elaborate on those topics. The first of these themes relates to memorable teachers.

Best Teacher

Most of the participants described their best teacher as the one who took the time to reach out and make them feel recognized, cared for, valued, or protected. The participants often saw this behavior as "above and beyond the call of duty." Some educators, parents, or counselors might argue that this was special treatment and as such was unnecessary or undesirable. However, virtually *all* the essays submitted suggest that solitary deaf or hard of hearing children experience ongoing and pervasive challenges to their self-esteem and confidence while attending local schools. The exceptional positive regard from certain teachers seems to have provided a necessary counterbalance—that of building or restoring self-esteem. Participants, such as the following, frequently mentioned that the encouragement they received from a single teacher remained with them for the duration of their academic careers.

> The best experience I ever had with a teacher was with my speech team coach in high school. He was always very supportive and encouraging and never told me he thought I couldn't do something. Even when I wanted to try out debate (which many teachers might discourage for a deaf child), he let me do it. He never tried to protect me from failure and always reminded me of my strengths. F 93

Another participant mentioned a debate team coach as well. The coach worked with her diligently, helping her to prepare for an upcoming event. As time drew near, she became more and more nervous about speaking in front of an audience and hearing the questions and comments made by other students. She begged the coach to excuse her from the event. He gave her a final boost of confidence when he looked her straight in the eye and said, "I see the person you really are. You are smarter than anyone in this school. I see past your hearing problems. I SEE YOU. Show people who you are, past your ears. Believe in yourself!"

It is obvious that this coach was creative as well as encouraging. He was willing to make allowances for the student's hearing loss. This represents an absence of the rigidity or ignorance that caused other teachers to go into the annals of "worst teachers," as will be shown later in this chapter. He gave the student an effective example of "reasonable accommodations," thus providing a very important lesson for her life. The student took her teacher's advice to heart, with the following results:

> I refused to worry about rebuttals. I just concentrated on speaking clearly. My partner wrote down points the other teams spoke on, and I argued our points back from all of my research, quoting this and that. We [were] county champs that year. I still have the award and pictures. I treasure them. From then on, I began to believe in myself, that I could figure my way out of tough spots.   F 84

I found it interesting that when describing their best teachers, participants often mentioned what these teachers did *not* do. They would also often say that their best teacher was "the only teacher" who did such and such. This suggests that these teachers were an exception rather than the rule; they stood out from the norm. Consider the following description of a favorite teacher:

> The best experience I had was with my high school English instructor. [He] was very aware of my deafness and took that into consideration while teaching. He made sure he taught facing the class so I could speechread him. [He] made sure not to mumble and never grew a mustache. [He] was very careful to explain the problems in my English papers so I understood

them. This was important to me, as most instructors had never taken the time to explain my errors.   F 81

Several participants spoke positively of teachers who encouraged them to teach their classmates about their hearing loss. They also recommended that children being mainstreamed as solitaries today do this as well. From the excerpts below, we can see that discussing one's hearing loss with classmates enhanced the self-esteem of the deaf or hard of hearing children and educated the teachers and students involved.

> This teacher was the only teacher I had who was genuinely interested in my hearing impairment. He would ask me questions and get me talking about it. We had to give speeches in that class, and he asked me to give a speech on hearing impairments and base it on my own experiences. I remember thinking that was the last thing I wanted to do, but I agreed to do it. And I believe from that moment on, things really changed for me in terms of being my own advocate and self-disclosing on my own.   F 91

Since the general public has so little information about deafness and its ramifications, we should not be surprised that participants emphasized the positive impact that conveying this information had on their relationships with their classmates.

> Co-teaching a class on disabilities was one of the best experiences I had ever had. [My teacher] allowed me to teach the class about hearing loss, demonstrate equipment, hearing aids, etc. It was a lot of fun and really opened eyes. This made me feel welcome and, in turn, the classmates respected me more, realizing there was more to me than they thought.   F 91

A few teachers had the foresight to use the deaf child's presentation as the basis for informing not just hearing students who were classmates of that child, but other children in the school as well. The first teacher described below tape-recorded the deaf student's presentation, and the second teacher had the student put her experiences in a newsletter. Both teachers provided creative opportunities for the deaf or hard of hearing child to explain his or her situation to classmates and demonstrate specific skills and the ability to make a contribution.

My teacher had me do a "deaf" presentation—[in which I had to] talk about my deafness, show the class fingerspelling, and have the class ask me questions relating to my deafness. This speech was tape-recorded so she could use it with her other classes.   F 87

My fourth grade teacher was sensitive to my difficulties working in a mainstreamed environment. She often had special activities for me that would help me to express my creativity and my communication. She encouraged me to write a newsletter to share with my peers. I think she provided these activities to help me feel more included in the class and to make my peers more aware of what I had to offer and what I could contribute. Being in her classroom was like an oasis in a hard, uncaring desert.   M 85

Some favorite teachers encouraged their deaf students to talk with them about any issues they might have been facing. The participants quoted below felt fortunate to have had a teacher who became a good friend, who was willing to help not only with homework but with personal problems as well.

This teacher took the time to help me with any problems I had, both those relating to English, as well as those relating to personal problems I exhibited during the school year. I knew I could always go to him when a problem arose, and he would be there to help me through it. [He] and I remained friends and discussed anything from deafness to personal problems. [He] was one of the few people I could trust to value my opinions and care for my feelings as a Deaf person.   F 81

It is clear from these responses that deaf or hard of hearing children, prone to social isolation, need more attention than hearing students from teachers, coaches, and other adults. These best teachers made sure that the other students were aware of positive ways to view and interact with the deaf or hard of hearing child, noticed the child's strong points and made sure everyone else was aware of them too, and gave him or her some extra encouragement to help counterbalance any negative experiences.

As for me, I don't have many specific memories about teachers. I recall with great gratitude that my elementary school teachers were very encouraging to me. I remember sitting on Mrs. White's lap, learning to read. I remember Mrs. Pickering singling out me and two guys to work on advanced arithmetic in third grade. I remember Miss Psaharris taking special interest in me because we both had Greek ancestors. All of them were easy to lipread, and it was easy for me to keep my straight-A average. All of these teachers deserve credit that my solitary experience in elementary school was as good as it was in the academic arena, at least.

Worst Teacher

Participants' stories about their worst teachers reminded me of one eighth grade teacher, who made a point of letting me know that I should not expect any special treatment. In fact, I felt that she saw it as her job to make my life more difficult than it already was. This particular teacher gave me enough trouble that my mother became angry and made an appointment for both of us to meet with her. I recall that the issue had to do with seating assignments, which my teacher insisted had to be in alphabetical order. She wanted students to read out loud in turn, in that alphabetical order I couldn't hear the other students and never knew where they were in the chapter when my turn to read came. My mother and I weren't asking for me to be excused from reading but to be allowed to read first so that I would not need to worry about following along with the other students. Yet, the teacher's attitude suggested that we were asking her to bend over backwards. In the following excerpt, a participant describes a similar experience.

> My worst experience was with an eighth grade social studies teacher who would not give me a front seat because, with a last name beginning with T, I belonged in the back right corner, and seating me in the front would ruin her beautiful alphabetical order. Insisting that I needed a front seat so that I could see the board and hear was to no avail. It took several trips to the principal's office to plead my case before she relented. F 69

Many of the worst teachers described by participants seemed to believe that the children didn't have an actual hearing loss but were faking or exaggerating the challenges they faced. I have often wondered if a hearing person could possibly imagine how that feels: to be told, "you're not really deaf, I know you are just trying to get away with something." Receiving such feedback from a teacher can make a child feel terribly and pervasively powerless. Imagine being so nearsighted that you couldn't read a sentence on the blackboard, but being told by a teacher that if you did not copy that sentence into your notebook you would receive a failing grade. That might give an inkling of what it feels like to be told you are faking a hearing loss.

> The worst experience I ever had was with a junior high basketball coach. From the beginning of the year, he never showed an interest in helping me. I remember going through the year in a daze of confusion, never really sure what was going on. When my parents came into school for a special meeting to express their concerns, he commented, "She hears what she wants to hear." He insisted that I was too smart to be deaf and that I was playing with everyone, audiological evidence to the contrary.   F 93

Quite a few participants talked about a teacher who was unwilling or unable to conceal the fact that he or she did not want to deal with a deaf child. This perceived sentiment was often mixed with the perception of low expectations.

> I worked extra hard in my high school art class because I thought art was one thing I could do on my own, and I really liked it. However, I never got over a D, and most of the time it was an F. I never understood this. When I would ask for help, the teacher would say she was too busy. One day, I went to class early and saw her telling another person that she hated when they put special education students in her class, so she automatically failed them. I was so hurt, I gave up my dream for art.   M 83

Some teachers were insensitive even to the deaf student's most basic communication needs. These teachers would talk while facing the blackboard or walking around the room, making it impossible for the deaf or hard of hearing child to read their lips. To make matters worse, these teachers sometimes demeaned and embarrassed the deaf and hard of hearing students in front of the entire class.

> Probably one of the most painful of my experiences was taking a major spelling test and flunking because I could not lipread single words out of context. After I tried to tell the teacher of my predicament, she scolded me in front of the entire class and then picked a peer to read the words to me in the back of the room during a retake. Because the class was still in ses-

sion, she whispered the words to me. Needless to say, I flunked the spelling test even though I knew how to spell every single word.   F 66

I had a fifth grade teacher who really didn't care if I didn't understand what she was teaching. She always moved around the classroom or faced the blackboard when she spoke. I remember reminding her to turn around to face me when she spoke. She responded, "If you didn't hear what I said . . . Tough!"   F 83

One time in high school, my teacher had to leave unexpectedly, so he tape-recorded his lecture for our class later that day. I felt frustrated sitting through the playing of that tape and not hearing a word. I felt quite annoyed with the teacher, as it was a complete waste of my time to be stuck in that room for an hour and a half, understanding nothing on the tape. And the other kids knew it too.   F 83

Some teachers would become angry if the children did not hear their names being called or if they missed some important information during a lecture. Or, they would conduct themselves in a blatantly unprofessional and unkind manner.

In the fourth grade, I gave a report on Wrigley Field but made the mistake of pronouncing Wrigley Field with a W sound. The teacher kept correcting me with an R sound, which I could not hear. Wrigley kept coming out with a W sound as the kids laughed and laughed. (I can still see their faces laughing.) That episode just decimated my self-esteem.   M 65

Once, I was working on a homework assignment in class, concentrating hard and oblivious to all sounds. Later, other students told me that my teacher had called my name several times, and when I did not respond, he lost patience and pretended to throw his stapler at me to get my attention. I was mortified to learn about this and imagined the other students seeing him do that.   F 80

This teacher would stand up and start speaking, and then all of a sudden, she would look at me and ask, "Can you hear me over there?" I remember wishing the ground would just open up and swallow me. I found this really embarrassing. While she may have been concerned about me, I felt she was drawing too much attention to it in front of my classmates. I was always nervous about when she would do it again.   F 91

Some teachers adopted a stance that since the deaf child would need to contend with unacceptable treatment in the "real world," she ought to learn to fend for herself.

> I was beaten up in this gym class three times. Kids laughed and called me "freak." This went on for months. I was deathly afraid of gym and found myself keeping close to any adult to ward off those bad kids. I asked the teacher to keep an eye on me, and that was met with rolled eyes. No help, no protection. The teacher just told me I had to get tough and deal with the "real world."   F 84

The worst teachers demonstrated their disdain, impatience, and inflexibility on a daily basis. As might be expected, such negative experiences had a lasting impact on the young people who bore the brunt of their ignorance.

> My worst teacher in grade school didn't care that I was deaf. He sat me in the back of the room where I couldn't possibly see him. He talked while facing the chalkboard so I could never speechread him, and he talked so fast that I would never understand what he was saying. He made me feel worthless. He made me feel like being deaf was a disease that he didn't want to catch. The experience turned me off to teachers for a while, as well as to education.   F 81

> One day, I missed something she said. She approached me and told me to sit properly. I complied, but she uttered the word "deaf-mute" in the most demeaning way. The class laughed at me. With this public humiliation, I felt this rage burning inside me. I don't know what I did to control myself at that moment. The years have passed, but I still have this rage against that woman.   M 85

Some readers will respond with compassion to these essay excerpts while others may feel that the school years are hard for everyone. It is true that the school years, especially middle school and high school, are fraught with possibilities for difficulties, failure, and personality conflicts with a teacher. However, hearing students, even those who have social difficulties, at least have the benefit of knowing what those around them are saying. They have a much greater chance of *knowing* where they stand, who their friends are, and which adults can be counted on for support or assistance. It is important to keep in mind that deaf and hard of hearing children are not privy to the fairly constant conversation going on around them. They are only privy to comments directed exclusively at them and thus have a more difficult time dealing with problems. Consequently, they are at a greater disadvantage when negative interactions occur.

Best Classmates and Friends

Most of the participants had both good and bad experiences with classmates. Several participants spoke about friends who seemed to embrace their hearing loss in a way that counteracted their sense of self-consciousness or shame.

> In fourth grade, I got an FM system,[2] and my friend was so excited that she wanted to wear it all the time! I remember cringing at the thought of having to wear these really big headphones, not wanting to be "different" in any way. And here she was, proud to be the poster girl for assistive technology! She would stay after school with me to put the system away and recharge the batteries. On weekends, she would encourage me to bring the system home so that we could "play" with it. She taught me at an early age to embrace my hearing loss and not be embarrassed by it.   F 87

Some female participants wrote of boyfriends who suggested that having a hearing loss was nothing to be ashamed of and that they not hide their hearing aids under their hair.

> I met my husband in high school. He was probably the first person besides my parents and speech teacher who I talked with about my deafness. When I told him that I wanted to pull my hair up but couldn't because of my hearing aids, he said, "Why not?" He convinced me that people would be more accommodating of my deafness if they could see my hearing aids. After this conversation, I was no longer afraid to reveal my hearing aids in public.   F 93

Often the best friends would act as "ears" for the deaf youngster, particularly in social situations.

> At a party, about twenty-five of us were playing a group game where there was a lot of talking. I have a really difficult time in situations like this. In

the game, each of us had to name something we did that we believed no one else in the room had ever done. If you guessed wrong, you were out of the game. Of course, I didn't catch any of this and was sitting there thinking, "Oh my goodness! What am I going to say when it comes to me? I have no idea what is going on here!" This girl came and sat beside me and asked if I knew what was going on. She filled me in and pretty much saved me right there. We became good friends after that.   F 91

Sometimes the deaf children's friends would invent creative ways to be of assistance.

This friend always spoke clearly and slowly. Plus, she wasn't afraid to write things down if I didn't understand. As we grew older and my speechreading skills became less reliable, I would carry around my TTY. And if I didn't understand her, she would type on it. She was careful to let me know what was going on around me, filling me in on the things she knew I couldn't hear.   F 81

Many participants spoke about a best friend who taught them different things about life, helped them in social situations where they didn't hear or understand what was going on, or stood up for them. These friends "filled them in" with important youth culture information, such as lyrics to popular songs.

My best experience was with the girl that lived next door to me. She taught me all the words to all the new music. We would sit in front of a stereo and play songs over and over while she would enunciate all the words. It meant a lot to be able to "sing" along to all the music.   F 85

I recall my own great desire, particularly in junior and senior high school, to know the lyrics to popular songs. Deaf and hard of hearing children and teenagers can frequently use their residual hearing to discern certain parts of music. It can be difficult for a hearing person to imagine what this is like. When I give lectures about hearing loss, I write on the board, "The cat in the hat is fat." Then, to demonstrate how a hard of hearing child would hear this phrase, I take an eraser and remove all the consonants, reducing the phrase to gibberish.

What did this mean for a deaf or hard of hearing person's ability to hear music? It means we hear *some* sounds in a musical composition, but not others. So when I listen to a CD, I hear *something* that I can enjoy. But it's not the same as what a hearing person would hear.

Even now, more than thirty-five years later, I know the lyrics to most Beatles songs. I also know the lyrics of many musicals, such as *West Side Story, My Fair Lady, Fiddler on the Roof,* and *The Fantastiks*. If I had the printed lyrics in front of me, I could often follow along with the music. If I did not have the printed lyrics while the music was playing, I would have no idea what the lyrics were. When I first arrived at Gallaudet, I found that this was yet another commonality I shared with many other deaf and hard of hearing individuals. My hearing loss is much worse today than when I attended high school; yet my ability to enjoy music, albeit limited, remains.

Several participants spoke positively of friends who encouraged them to get involved with any manner of extracurricular activity.

> My best friend would always stand up for me. He would tell me what everyone else was talking about if I missed something (which was often) in conversations among hearing peers. He encouraged me to be involved with the band and sports. He helped to make my mainstreaming experience a positive one.   M 93

In my own mid-elementary summer months, I would often ride my bike over to a nearby neighborhood playground. This was ideal for me because maybe six to ten kids would be there each day. Most of the time, we would be outside. The smaller number of kids meant that they could get to know my skills more easily. And it was quieter, so I could more easily follow any one-on-one conversations.

We usually played physical games, and I was good at all of them. I have very positive memories of those times. Once, when choosing sides for baseball, a particular boy was a little reluctant to accept me on his team. Then I hit a home run my first time up to bat. From that point on, he would call me "the girl slugger" with obvious admiration. (I could *see* the admiration on his face.) After those few summers, I never saw him again until we were both adults in our thirties. He still remembered me, as I did him! This one boy's positive remark was an internalized source of support for me during all my solitary years and beyond as well.

The participants talked about classmates who were particularly supportive with academic experiences as well. These friends repeated the words during spelling tests, shared notes, or helped out during group discussion situations.

> My sixth grade teacher had a very thick accent. I knew right away that she wasn't going to be easy to lipread. My friends in the class were helpful. They would often turn to me and [repeat what the teacher said]. Them, I could lipread. One boy, my best friend at the time, was great. Spelling tests were the worst. But after the teacher said the word and the class wrote the word down, this friend would turn to me and repeat it for me. If I still could not understand the word, he was the only one who was willing to get out of his seat and act it out. He was a very outgoing and brave fellow. I appreciated his efforts.   F 87

Lastly, several participants described situations where friends stood up for them when they were being teased or bullied.

> My friend and I were involved in many activities together—dancing, Girl Scouts, sports. One time, I was walking home from school and someone started to beat me up. My friend popped up and pulled the kid right off of me. From that time on, she always walked home with me so no one could tease or pick on me. I was so grateful for that.   F 83

> This friend and I did homework together from third to fifth grade. He saw me as equal and treated me kindly. He defended me and told the class bully to leave me alone.   M 88

Many participants believed that having at least one good friend was a critical factor in surviving those school days. As I read through the many e-mails I received, I thought of my own classmates in my K–12 and college years—those who made my life easier. My friends at elementary school were Mary Ellen and Bettina. We lived very near each other and had become friends as soon as we were old enough to play outside unsupervised, which was pretty young in Cos Cob in the 1950s. In the elementary years, they were "it," so to speak. In junior high, senior high, and at Washington College, I did manage to have one or two close friends. If not for these women, life would have indeed been terribly lonely.

Worst Classmate

Despite having certain teachers and peers as anchors of a sort, many participants struggled with low self-esteem throughout their school years. They shared a seemingly endless litany of negative social experiences. While space does not allow me to include more than a handful of their stories, I hope this will not lessen the impression that such experiences, reported by virtually all the participants, were painful, ongoing, and had a lasting impact.

> The worst fellow student experience is hard to identify because I had many such experiences. Students teased and laughed. They would sarcastically whine that they couldn't have "radios in their ears" like me. They would talk with their back towards me or cover their mouth and challenge me to understand them. Nothing stands out in my mind as the "worst" experience, as they were all pretty bad. From all the teasing and ridicule, I concluded that I was worthless and that deafness was really a curse.   F 81

> The boys in sixth grade thought it was cool to make fun of the way I talked. Often there were no teachers around to stop them. They would make fun of me right to my face, and the other girls were just giggling. It was a very isolating and humiliating experience, and I would often go home and cry. F 93

It is interesting to note that some fellow students adopted the attitude that the deaf child was only pretending not to hear. I wonder if they picked this attitude up from a teacher like some of those described earlier.

> In eighth grade, the girls complained to the teacher that I'm a liar, that I'm not really deaf because I can hear with the hearing aids. The girls then would test me by calling my name behind me. I would hear them yelling so I would turn my head around. Then the girls said to the teacher, "See we told you. She is not deaf!" I ran out of the class crying. Junior high days were the worst!   F 66

Some experiences reflected a cruel and provocative form of persecution. In the few stories where participants confessed to retaliating, the deaf or hard of hearing children were the ones who were ultimately punished.

> The worst experience is tragically easiest to remember. It was probably in seventh grade. One day, I'd had an especially bad day of "teasing" (persecution would be a better word for their treatment) by a group of boys (who were also from my neighborhood) who were particularly malicious toward me. Toward the end of the day, I'd basically had enough of them and wasn't feeling too good. In math class, we were doing individual work. I was working on my problems when one boy got up and went to sharpen his pencil. As he passed behind me, he tapped me with his pencil. It shouldn't have bothered me, but I was already hurt and seething. I recall thinking, "If he does that again, I don't know what I will do." Sure enough, he came back and tapped me again, and I shot out of my chair, and stabbed him with my pencil a few times. Luckily, I didn't seriously hurt him, but I did get suspended for it.   M 81

Bullying has always been problematic, and we know from media reports and recent research that it continues to be common today. Deaf children are particularly vulnerable even to apparent "generic bullying." In other words, they are simply more likely to be bullied.

> One student bullied me frequently. He would be riding his bike on the school grounds and punch me on the shoulder as he passed by me. I eventually got fed up with his antics and tried to attack him, but he pinned me down on the grass. He was Chinese and knew karate. Good thing I didn't get hurt badly. My mom and dad would sometimes call his parents to stop him from bullying me. This would work for a short time, but then he would be back to his old habits. This was pretty much a regular occurrence between sixth grade and eighth grade.   M 88

Tormented similarly to this boy, one female participant was involved in a situation where her family took the perpetrator to court. Unfortunately, this was to no avail.

> One boy took special delight in daily torture. This was made worse by the indifference of the teacher. This boy took pleasure in striking my head,

especially from behind. (To this day, if a person comes up behind me to tap on my shoulder or get my attention, I will nearly come out of my skin with fright.) We took this kid to court, and the mom refused to show up several times. So, the judge threw out the assault charges. At school, the kid continued to taunt me by saying, "Nothin' you can do to get me." And, it sure was that way—from the teacher to the principal to the court system. It was a very bad time.   F 84

Reading these stories brought back some painful memories of my own. As I read the bullying reports, I thought, "I guess I was fortunate to not be bullied too much." Then I wondered, "How much bullying is too much?" How can I compare the amount of bullying I experienced with that of someone else?

As previously mentioned, I had two friends on Mead Avenue, Mary Ellen and Bettina, who remain my friends to this day. There was another girl in the neighborhood, however, who took it upon herself to make my life miserable. She never became my friend, even though all four of us lived on the same small block throughout our K–12 years. This girl would regularly convince Mary Ellen and Bettina not to play with me. When they were "on her side," they would tell me lies that exploited my hearing loss, like "Gina your mother is calling you," and then they would run off and play without me. Or, they would hide in the bushes and yell my name, knowing that I would hear the yelling but not be able to figure out from which direction their voices were coming.

One particular incident burns in my brain. I was nine or ten years old. A deep pipe trench had been dug alongside my house. Mary Ellen, Bettina, and I would talk about how much fun it would be to play in that trench, although we knew that was probably forbidden. One day, they told me they had to go do their homework. A while later, from my bedroom window upstairs, I saw them running in that ditch with that other girl. I was so hurt and angry that I retaliated against their trickery by using a long rope to tie their three bicycles together in a most complicated manner. I am sure the rage I felt was similar to that of the boy who retaliated against the bully with a pencil. He used a pencil, I used a piece of rope.

Somehow I remained friends with Mary Ellen and Bettina. I am not sure exactly how that happened. I think I waited a few weeks and just went over to their house, or they came to mine, and we were friends again. But nothing was ever said about those incidents. After the rope incident, they never ostracized me again. The troublemaker was (mercifully for me) not around during our junior high years; she went away to a private school or lived elsewhere for a while.

To this day, I wonder why she engaged in this form of bullying. It bothered me enough that when it came time for my twentieth high school reunion, I made a point to ask her if she remembered these incidents. She said she didn't, so I dropped the issue. Still, I wonder.

In the following excerpt, the young girl was not specifically teased for her hearing loss but was singled out for ostracism because of her differentness.

> I was invited to a sleep-over birthday party in the fourth or fifth grade, attended by the most popular girls in my class. My mother had bought me a new outfit for the occasion and I was excited. Late in the evening, for some reason, the group of girls turned on me. I'm not sure how it happened but one of them stepped on my head as I was sleeping, and this was soon followed by another act of physical violence. I remember the girl whose party it was asking me, "Does it bother you when people are so mean to you?"
>
> F 93

What is a child to do when beset with such odds? I actually hosted a slumber party when I was in the sixth grade, knowing full well that it would be a difficult situation for me because the girls would talk incessantly in the dark. Regardless, my desire to fit in was so intense that I didn't care about that. I just wanted them to like me for inviting them to my party.

This was the first of actually several parties I hosted fully cognizant that I would not be a part of my own party! I am almost embarrassed to tell of these attempts to fit in: They reek of the lack of disclosure that pervaded my life, an example set by my father and the time and place in which we lived. Today, I think of these attempts as pitiful. I really hope that deaf and hard of hearing children today don't feel compelled to become complicit with such pretense.

In sixth grade, there were several girls in school who I really wanted to befriend. They were a tight-knit group, and one day they "let me" sit with them in the cafeteria. I clearly remember being so excited at the possibility of being let into their circle. At the same time, I was frightened that they wouldn't like me. I convinced my mother to let me have that slumber party. I distinctly remember one day at lunch asking, "Would you like to come to a slumber party at my house?" They looked at each other and giggled and laughed, and then said yes.

Later, at the actual slumber party, the five or six girls, whom I invited and really wanted to be friends with, stayed up all night talking while I laid in the dark, hearing their voices but not understanding one word they said.

That sixth grade party was not the worst of it. As a teenager I held at least three parties that I can remember where I invited all the "cool kids" even though I was not one of them. They would come to my house (or to where I was babysitting), and proceeded to party in their usual way. I was left alone. They were all paired off, doing what high school kids do at parties. I would busy myself with setting up food, putting away food, getting more food, or pretending I had something to do upstairs. For the entire party. I tried to escape the stark difference between their paired off activities and my solitary hostess role by frantically keeping busy.

Deaf, But Definitely Not Dumb

The phrase *deaf and dumb* was used historically to mean "deaf and cannot speak." In the 1800s, even Deaf adults proudly referred to themselves as "deaf-mutes," and the word *mute* referred to their love for their native sign language. However, over time, the term *dumb* has come to connote *stupid* rather than *mute*, and thus the terminology has fallen in with racial slurs and gone the way of other politically incorrect descriptors. Regardless, two participants included this terminology in their responses. My guess is that the term is still tossed around today.

In fourth (or sixth grade), I arrived to class one day just before the bell and before the teacher was there. I noticed that kids were standing around giggling, and on the blackboard in six-inch letters was: D. D. D. D. D. D.

After a few minutes of asking around, I was told that it stood for Dumb [my name] Duh, Duh, Duh. I never really found out who did it, but the combination of that discovery and the memory of the giggling really hurt me to the core for many years.   F 70

One female student apparently felt that the best way to be accepted in the gang of popular students was to be a bully. Several horrible scenes come to mind, like her breaking in my gym locker to retrieve my jacket that contained my hearing aids and batteries. She actually stood up in front of class to say I have the DD hearing aids and batteries. The DD stands for deaf and dumb.   F 83

These are some of the stories told by sixty adults who were mainstreamed as solitaries. These stories prompted my own stories and will likely prompt more stories in any former or current solitary who reads them. They represent much about our lives in the hearing world. It is not to say that we do not have hearing family members and friends that are dear to us. It is just to say that we have had some pretty distressing experiences caused by a pervasive and longstanding ignorance.

4

But Mom, I Hate Telling People!

DISCLOSURE refers to the practice of deaf or hard of hearing people informing hearing people that they have a hearing loss. It is a term used when talking about interfacing with the world, and it is generally used by those who either spend ample time as a solitaire (either in the workplace or in social settings) or by groups who advocate such. Truthfully, a child who is educated as a solitaire needs to know what, how, and when to disclose. For a child to tell another child or even an adult "I'm deaf" or "I'm hard of hearing" often does little to change the nature of the interchange. But if a child says, "I'm deaf; let's converse on e-mail," or "I'm hard of hearing; if we move away from the crowd, I will be able to hear you better," the disclosure may accomplish something in the deaf or hard of hearing child's favor.

My earliest experience with disclosure happened on my first day of first grade. While waiting to enter the school building, my fellow students noticed that my hearing aid was strapped to my chest with a harness. They asked, "What's that?" And when I said, "It's a hearing aid," they would yell, "Can you hear me?" directly into the microphone sitting on my chest. Or they would snicker and laugh. My mother soon realized that I should put the harness inside my blouse so no one would see the hearing aid. Although she did this to protect me, the message sent—hide the hearing aid, hide the hearing loss—was not altogether positive.

Many years later, I realized that I had no idea how my father reacted to the discovery of my hearing loss. I asked my mother about this, and her response was, "Well, he didn't want you to have a hearing aid." We talked about this a bit and concluded that he was concerned that the hearing aid would make the hearing loss obvious and that the other children would tease me about it. Truth be told, he was right on both counts. It was obvious, the kids made fun of me, and I quickly learned to hate the hearing aid and to make every effort to hide both the aid and my hearing loss.

Once I had been at Gallaudet for a few years, my approach to disclosure started to change. When I began disclosing, my parents' reactions surprised me. At Christmas during the mid-70s, I found myself trapped at the dinner table with the adults, and as usual, I could not follow any of the conversation. Having been at Gallaudet for several years by this time, I was becoming bolder in handling such situations. When I noticed that my nieces and nephews were collecting their ice skates and preparing to go skating at the neighborhood pond, I decided to join them.

When my mother noticed me getting my skates ready, she was clearly upset with me for choosing to go play with the kids, and sternly told me to stay with the adults. I remember being very surprised because I thought she would understand my choice. I always assumed that she knew how little I could grasp during group conversations. But she acted as if she was embarrassed by my behavior. Maybe someone else in the room had made a comment about me. To this day, I do not know what prompted her reaction, but it told me that she really didn't understand how difficult those family gatherings were for me.

So, for me to decide to go ice skating was a kind of disclosure. It was indirect, I admit. At age twenty-five, it was all I could do to save myself from that dreaded after-dinner blabbering. Not to say that what they were talking about was blabbering or unimportant, but it was Greek to me. By my actions, I was saying to my family, "You already know I cannot hear. I don't want to sit here while you all talk in your usual way." My mother's rejection of that choice, in a way, was a rejection of disclosure as well as a rejection of my unwillingness to "just sit there and act normal," as my father always did.

A few years later, an incident with my father sadly revealed some of the repressed emotions that resulted from life as a solitaire. It also further illustrates my gradual breaking away from my father's manner of disclosure and my search for a different manner that would improve communication between me and the individuals to whom I disclosed.

My mother had decided to host a family reunion at our Cos Cob home. Having been at Gallaudet for almost ten years, I had not seen my aunts, uncles, and cousins for at least that long. I looked forward to the occasion but was also struck with trepidation. What would it be like for me? Would I just eat and pretend to be listening, laughing when they laughed? Thinking about it gave me a knot in my stomach.

Then I had an idea. I decided to tell each relative that I would like to interview them in a quiet corner to learn what they had been doing over the past decade. I also wanted to share this information with my father. I had to muster some courage, wondering if they would think it was a silly idea. When the day came, to my happy surprise, they were very willing. My relatives and I went into the living room or upstairs to chat for a spell—away from the *Big Fat Greek Wedding*–like chatter. I took notes to later share with my Dad. I had a feeling my father was wondering what I was doing, but he didn't say anything at the time.

The next day, Dad, Mom, and I were having dinner, and out of the blue, he asked, "So what were you doing yesterday with that notebook?" I was hopeful that he would be interested and pleased to learn about my adventure. "Well, let me go get the notebook and I will show you," I replied. I retrieved the notebook and opened it up on the dinner table. When I showed him the notes about each relative, I said, "I told them that you and I would miss out on the conversation, so I wanted to find out what they had been doing for the last ten years, and that I would share it with you as well."

He was quiet for a moment. Then he said tersely, "You don't have to speak for me." I replied, "Well, I wasn't really speaking you; I wanted the information myself." He then repeated, now with anger, "You do not have to speak for me." I said, "Well I am sorry. I didn't mean to speak for you, but I really am tired of not knowing what is going on." Full of anger, he stood up and yelled, "Don't you EVER speak for me again." My angry reply caused him to turn over the kitchen table—plates, food, and all! Then he ordered me out of the house and told me to never come back.

I know I did those interviews for me. Why did I say it was for Dad also? Because I didn't think doing it for myself was a good enough reason? Because I wanted to divulge and stop the deception? Because I was subconsciously hoping Dad would see that there were other acceptable ways to deal with his hearing loss?

I am not sure—but perhaps it was a combination of these reasons. Eventually Dad and I reconciled. We never spoke of the incident, however.

Several other experiences helped me to recognize that disclosure can take different forms. When I received the invitation to my tenth high school reunion in 1978, I read it with sadness as well as anxiety, thinking how nice it would be to go but knowing I did not have the courage to do so. I still had that sense of not having contributed anything. I still felt badly that my high school classmates never got to know me. I was afraid that they might have negative views about d/Deaf people or that they would ignore me at the reunion. I was not willing to take the risk of putting myself in such a vulnerable position. In addition, the single classmate with whom I was still in touch did not plan to attend. So, I trashed the invitation with some regret but with recognition that I was obviously not ready to venture back into that world.

By 1988, however, it occurred to me that if I brought an interpreter, the reunion might at least be an interesting experience. I sent a letter to the planning committee and asked if they would waive the interpreter's dinner fee. They agreed, which I found very encouraging. Thus, with a graciously willing friend/interpreter, I decided to take this gamble and attend the reunion. In retrospect, I realize that this was an act of disclosure, albeit a different kind of disclosure than any to which I had ever been exposed. I was taking an interpreter to a social event for pure, unadulterated, personal reasons.

Lo and behold, it was a wonderful, affirming experience. The first night involved a dinner dance and cocktail hour. I felt a little funny entering that hotel with my friend Renate. I had no idea if anyone would recognize me, much less make an effort to talk to me. The event was rather formal, and only a few people talked to me, but I still found it interesting to see what everyone looked like!

By going to the reunion with an interpreter, I was disclosing. I was not directly saying, "I am hard of hearing. Please talk louder." I was showing by my actions that I was a user of sign language. In the blurb that we were asked to submit for the program book, about what we had been doing since high school, I had mentioned my work at Gallaudet. These were my first official acts of disclosure to my high school classmates. To them I was saying, "I am deaf. I have learned sign language, and thus I have brought an interpreter with me." It was yet another symbolic breaking away from the nondisclosing example my father had set.

Despite this initial disclosure, I only spoke to a handful of old classmates that first night. The next day, however, included a picnic at the nearby beach, and it was there that several classmates came up to me and said things that just made my decade, so to speak. One particularly sensitive guy confessed that all during junior and senior high, he had known I had some kind of problem but didn't realize how severe it was. Then he said he was sorry he had not befriended me! A group of guys who used to be in a band that played at numerous high school dances told me that they had always agreed amongst themselves that I was the best dancer at their shows. Wow! Talk about an ego boost. Those remarks made me feel wonderful. To top this all off, one female classmate introduced herself to me in sign language, explaining that she worked with d/Deaf clients in a hospital setting. She and I have kept in touch ever since. It was a very special day for me, and I felt that my willingness to leave my comfort zone had paid off immeasurably.

This may all sound trivial to the average hearing person. But I felt that my total disconnection from my high school peers had been remedied in that one day. I felt like finally they knew who I was and why I had always been so quiet and withdrawn. Now at least some of them know that I am not shy or stupid or odd; I am just deaf. My method of disclosing had worked. It enabled me to interact to a previously impossible degree. It felt great.

At my twentieth high school reunion with two guys from the band that played at our school dances.

My college reunions have been another story altogether. I have yet to summon the nerve to attend a college reunion. I was only at Washington College for three years and only knew a few students well. In Greenwich, on the other hand, some of the high school classmates had also been elementary school classmates. I suspect that my college years were more painful, and thus there is greater emotional risk involved in venturing into that area.

Not Home Alone: A Surprising Strategy for Successful Disclosure

Over the years, I have taken many trips alone. In the 1980s and 1990s, most of my traveling was work related. I would add a few days or even a week to a trip to go sightseeing. The most memorable parts of these trips have been my nature walks. Some of my favorite hikes have been along the cliffs in Del Mar, California, the road between Diamond Head and Waikiki Beach on Oahu, Hawaii, the hills of Palo Alto, and neighborhoods in Boise, Idaho, Portland (both Oregon and Maine), and Great Barrington, Massachusetts.

More recently, I have taken quite a few road trips simply to engage my love for nature and novelty. A trip I took to Maine during the summer of 2001 illustrates a point related to disclosure. I had been to the island of Vinalhaven years before and found it to be a great place to ride a bike and a safe place for a woman traveling alone. I arrived on Vinalhaven with only my new twenty-one-speed hybrid bike, my knapsack, and a handlebar pack. I rode off the ferry, feeling somewhat like a beast of burden, and proceeded to make my way toward the bed-and-breakfast where I would spend my first three nights. At a confusing, unmarked intersection, a couple on single-speed bicycles with fat tires and fat seats were stopped. I called out to them, asking if they knew which road would lead me to the Fox Island Inn. They both pointed "thataway" and off I went with my considerable but manageable load, up the hill to my home for the next three days.

I had selected this particular bed-and-breakfast because my research had revealed that the owner allowed her guests to fix small meals in her kitchen. So, on that first evening, I was putting together a salad and some crackers, while a young woman from the bedroom across the living room was opening a can of soup. She smiled. I smiled. It was very quiet. An island out in the middle of the ocean. No cars going by. No hum from an air conditioner. No cell phones or TV. Very quiet indeed. She kept making eye contact and then looking away. Finally, I said, "Thanks for giving me directions." Then she said something. I didn't hear her. I mustered some courage and said, "I have a hearing impairment; if you could talk a bit louder it would help." She looked at me for what seemed like a long time, as if she were mustering her own courage as well. Then, very clearly with this cute hopeful look on her face, she said, "When we saw you on your fancy bike, I told my husband you must be a professional!" I laughed, and from that point on, Madeline and I conversed easily and pleasantly every time we were in the kitchen together.

Soon I met her friend Ted and learned that he had a Deaf friend with whom he often engaged in outdoor activities. They lived outside Philadelphia, and this Deaf man happened to be the only person Ted knew who enjoyed such activities. So, we had lots to talk about for three strangers thrown into a remote inn on an even more remote island.

I was continuously struck by the ease with which I could hear them and read their lips. Actually, if they spoke directly to each other, I did not understand them. But, they both paid ample attention to speaking directly to me. And it seemed that I rarely had to ask them to repeat anything. It was so pleasant and fun, and we quickly became friends. I have not seen them since that visit to Vinalhaven, but perhaps some day we will meet again.

Madeline and Ted were not the only hearing people I met and conversed with on that trip. I met others on Vinalhaven and several on the nearby island of Monhegan as well. Perhaps the simple lesson here is that disclosure can work if the surrounding environment is quiet and the hearing people are willing to modify their behavior as needed to enable conversation.

My last conversation during the trip was with a professional photographer who was on the same ferry with me returning from Monhegan. I had been intrigued watching him photograph a child on the boat. When we reached the dock, I mustered some more of that courage and asked if he had succeeded in getting the photographs he wanted. This started a conversation, and soon I learned that he knew of Gallaudet, having worked in Washington for a number of years. He asked some questions about sign language and d/Deaf people. I shared with him my observation that people in Maine were much more willing to slow down and speak clearly than people in Washington D.C. Together we pondered whether the relative peace and quiet of Maine had contributed to my ease of conversation as well. I wondered aloud, "If I'd had my husband or a friend with me, and we were seen conversing in sign language, would people still make the effort to talk to me?" The photographer replied, "Well, I don't think I would." I asked him why. "Well, I am ashamed to admit this," he said, "but I think I would have had this idea—and I admit it's erroneous and arrogant—that you were somehow lacking in . . . intelligence. And of course, the truth would be I don't have a clue about sign language."

It was so interesting to hear this friendly, honest man's admission. It affirmed my belief that uncomplimentary attitudes about sign language and d/Deaf people remain with us to this day. I wonder if our encounter led this photographer to examine his general beliefs about d/Deaf people, or if he has, even subconsciously, held on to the attitude that most d/Deaf people are not intelligent. I wonder if he is still thinking, wherever he is, that I was an exception to the rule.

My next stop on this particular trip allowed for an interesting juxtaposition. I drove to Cape Cod and spent several days with my sister Kathy and her family. Their house is not far from the Cape Cod Rail Trail, and I wanted to see how far I could get on that ingenious byway. I pedaled for maybe an hour and then turned around and retraced my path. Somehow I missed my exit from the trail and became lost. I rode back and forth for a stretch and could not figure out where I had gone wrong. I was tired, thirsty, and had to use the bathroom; it was time to ask for directions. Wouldn't you know it, when I asked one woman for directions, I could not understand a word she said. She spoke fast, in that manner we Deaf people sometimes call "puppet-mouth." I said, "I have a hearing impairment. Could you repeat that more slowly?" Disclosure got me nowhere this time; she did not modify her manner of speaking one iota. I said, "Thanks a lot" and rode in the direction she was pointing. Soon I saw someone else and stopped to ask for directions again. Same predicament. Same disclosure. Same result. I thought, "Isn't this something? Just one more reason to move to Maine!"

Granted, this is not exactly scientific evidence of a proven fact, as humorist Dave Barry would say. But I am pretty certain that the next time I travel to parts north, I will have similar experiences. I highly recommend that some other deaf or hard of hearing adventurers test my theory and write about their experiences.

Solitaires' Experience with Disclosure

Few of the Solitary Mainstream Project participants mentioned in their initial responses whether or not they talked about their hearing loss with significant others. However, the analysis technique I was using required another person to read the data and verify that the common themes I identified from their responses were comprehensive. This reader will ideally hold different views than the primary researcher. I invited Brenda Battat, an executive with

Self Help for Hard of Hearing, Inc., to serve in this capacity. For hard of hearing people, and particularly those who belong to self-advocacy groups, disclosure is a very important coping mechanism. These groups encourage their members to disclose their hearing loss with those they converse with, and more importantly, to educate about strategies hearing people can use to make themselves more comprehensible to a hard of hearing listener. I was not surprised therefore, when, upon reading the initial responses, Brenda commented, "They didn't disclose; that's very important!"

Working at Gallaudet University and being involved in the Deaf community had caused me to forget the impact of disclosure (or lack thereof) on life in the mainstream. In essence, there is very rarely reason to disclose a hearing loss at Gallaudet. However, if one is uncertain of another's hearing status, it is considered quite acceptable to ask, "Are you deaf or hearing?" That Brenda took note of this issue was significant, so I decided to ask the participants to elaborate on it with the following prompt:

> Tell me about how often (or how rarely) you disclosed your hearing loss to others in school. Did you disclose to teachers? To peers? To a counselor? What was that like? How often did you talk with someone about your hearing loss and/or related needs? How did others respond to your sharing? (This could range from reminding peers "Remember, I can't hear you when you are all talking at the same time" to speaking with your counselor for an hour every week about the issues you were facing.) Did you talk to parents or siblings about issues related to your hearing loss, and if so, how often? Try to give me the breadth and depth of your experience—even if just to say, "I never talked to anyone about my hearing loss, and here's why." Do you think the amount of or quality of disclosure was optimal (just perfect, not enough, not deep enough, whatever)? Can you think of anything that could have made it better for you? What can parents and schools do to help today's children address their hearing loss and their needs in the solitary mainstream environment?

Effort To Lipread vs. Resignation To Daydream

The majority of the participants responded that they did not disclose, and that, in fact, they dreaded disclosing. The following is a typical answer:

I remember clearly never wanting to tell people or announce the fact that I couldn't hear. I hated people to know because I felt it singled me out, and I hated the fact that it made me different. When I did end up telling people, it was often something that was mumbled out of a desperate realization that I had to say something so I wouldn't be considered rude or stupid. Often, I remember a sense of shame in telling people, a sense of embarrassment. I also recall being uncertain how to define myself. Am I hard of hearing? Am I hearing impaired? I'm not deaf because I don't know sign language. But I can't hear, so what am I? I hated calling myself hearing impaired, as it implied something was wrong with me, and I already was defensive that I couldn't hear. Being hard of hearing, to me, was always something associated with old people. In my mind, when I said I was hard of hearing, I suddenly became old. F 87

It is interesting to note that the participant was concerned that her lack of disclosure would cause people to assume that she was rude or stupid. Wouldn't it be better if, upon noticing that someone who is looking the other way has ignored a comment, an individual's first thought was "Oh, I wonder if this person is deaf!"

The same participant continues:

When I did tell people, it was often to say, "I need to lipread you, so please look at me when you talk." For some reason, this always held an element of attraction, as it wasn't so threatening. Lipreading was "cool." A fellow student would say, "Wow! You can't hear me but you can lipread me?" Games would be started out of such an exchange, and I would be popular and cool with that person for a little while. F 87

So kids thought lipreading was cool? Imagine if teachers were aware of this and capitalized on this interest? Why not teach all children to lipread? Why not have silent spelling bees where the students would have to read the teacher's lips? The teacher could throw in an element of charades or a similar game, so that students would have more information with which to identify selected words.

Many participants talked about spending a lot of time daydreaming or doodling because they couldn't follow along with the class. This coping skill went hand in hand with the lack of disclosure.

It's dumbfounding to remember some of this: sitting in classes day-dreaming, reading the homework, just being off in a daze somewhere or actually really trying hard to understand what was going on around me. But it was all mumbo jumbo. I had the classic "eyes glazed over" look every single day.   F 87

This is a behavior that parents and teachers should be able to spot, and it would behoove the adults to not ignore this warning sign. However, I wonder if concerned adults have a tendency to ignore obvious daydreaming in a deaf or hard of hearing child because they do not know how to remedy the situation. In other words, the child witnesses adults ignoring their daydreaming and learns to pretend that there is no problem. The lack of disclosure by adults would naturally influence a lack of disclosure among children, as my parents' lack of disclosure surely influenced me. Ignoring this behavior appears to the child as a form of pretense, as hiding the problem.

The following quote illustrates a child's acceptance of this need to feign normalcy while at once recognizing the ineffectiveness of this way of dealing with the world.

My most basic memory was a sense of not wanting people to know at all (but realizing they needed to know if I was to get by) and a sense of shame and embarrassment when I had to tell people. I would wonder, "Why can't I do sign language? Why do I try so hard to pretend I'm hearing when I can't hear?" There was a lot of pretense going on.   F 89

Happy To Explain Their Hearing Loss

A small handful of participants said they enjoyed telling people about their hearing loss and consequently, about themselves. One participant saw his hearing loss as a uniqueness, something of which to be proud. This perception enabled him to freely discuss his challenges as well as his triumphs.

I never had a problem disclosing my hearing loss to anyone. When asked, I simply took the opportunity to teach others about hearing loss, hearing aids, and the sense of pride I achieved overcoming the obstacles I faced. The end result of this interaction has been close friendships and a mutual sense of respect for individual differences. M 93

Several participants elaborated on the idea of encouraging children to educate others about their hearing loss. Others felt that the responsibility for this education lies with parents and teachers, not the child. Sharing certain information about one's hearing loss with others could be empowering for a deaf child; however, parents and teachers must discern when such would be the case. Especially with younger children, adults need to carefully evaluate when such self-advocacy efforts would be overwhelming or embarrassing.

Regardless of how active a role they have in educating teachers and peers, deaf or hard of hearing children must be able to freely and comfortably talk about their hearing loss whenever the need arises. The following comments are from a participant who did little disclosing during her K–12 years.

> I feel that it would benefit any child to be able to discuss it all the time, if needed. Maybe just bringing it up now and then at the supper table as part of the family chatter. Make it just part of the family, like Jane is deaf and John has freckles. It should be easier nowadays, now that more and more children with differing disabilities and diverse backgrounds are in the mainstream school environment. F 90

Parental encouragement indeed can significantly foster an environment where the subject of deafness is acknowledged rather than avoided. One participant attributes her very positive schooling experience to her parents' ability and willingness to do just that. Her resulting sense of security promoted her lifelong ability to comfortably discuss her deafness.

> When I was in elementary school, many kids would ask me how much I could hear. This became a game to us. They would ask me if I could hear their voices, a car passing, the school bell ringing, etc. And I would always answer, "No." They were fascinated with the fact that I couldn't hear. They would still continue asking me whether I heard certain sounds, no matter how often I told them I couldn't. As I grew older and entered middle school and high school, the kids would ask me how I lost my hearing. I was always

more than happy to explain how I became deaf. . . . I never felt like I did not belong. . . . I know without a doubt that my parents are responsible for the fact that I feel very secure about myself. They always made themselves available to me and supported me in everything. . . . We would talk a lot about technology and what I needed to make my life easier. My parents were knowledgeable about technologies available for deaf people and would always buy them for me. I have always had excellent communication with my parents throughout my life, and I feel that that is the most important tool a deaf child can have. F 93

A few fortunate participants explained that they never had to disclose; people in their surroundings already knew about their hearing loss. Generally, this was because they lived in a small town or attended a small school, and their parents always did the disclosing for them.

Not Like THOSE Deaf People!

Unfortunately, most of the Solitary Mainstream Project participants did not have such a positive experience with disclosure. Rather, the responses show the participants' pervasive sense of shame. One participant said she was confused about who was at fault for this sense of shame. Was it her fault for being too embarrassed to disclose her deafness to others, or was it her parents' fault?

It was not something we discussed in my family. Was it a secret? Was it shameful? I don't know. I just know that I was not at all comfortable discussing it. I most certainly did not talk about it enough while growing up! I wished it had been a more open topic for discussion in my family. Maybe it was, and I was too embarrassed or ashamed to discuss it, and therefore my parents left it alone. F 87

One source of this shame is illustrated by responses that focused on the participants' childhood desire to avoid being associated with other deaf or hard of hearing children.

I was uncomfortable and afraid of meeting other deaf people because they were like me, and I guess I didn't want to be deaf (during childhood, anyway). I didn't want to be handicapped. They waved their hands in the air and made funny sounds. I was not exposed to sign language in all its glory as a child, so I guess those waving hands were scary to me. The deaf people I met "talked funny" when they used speech, and I guess that was scary to me too. But in my heart, I knew they were deaf and I was deaf. But I wasn't like THAT! I didn't want to be like THAT! I didn't want to be lumped in with THEM. It was like looking in a mirror. Being with them would be admitting I was deaf too, and deaf people *were viewed as flawed in the hearing world where I lived.* F 95

In addition to mentioning their own early exposure to comments or nonverbal information that told them deafness was shameful, some participants expressed anger at their parents and/or other adults for the impact this message had on their lives and their choices. How horribly difficult it can be for a child to reconcile two conflicting messages: "You are smart, you are OK!" and "That other deaf kid; yes, he is deaf like you, but he is a dolt!"

Until I was fifteen and a half, I was afraid to meet or be associated with deaf and hard of hearing people. My parents raised me orally and did not expose me to other deaf and hard of hearing individuals, so I had no connection with them. I was terribly lonely and had all but accepted this fate. Once in awhile, we would come across other kids my age that were deaf and hard of hearing, and my parents would steer me away. They always had other problems in addition to their deafness, like retardation, spinal bifida (being confined to a wheelchair), drooling, making uncontrollable noises, Down syndrome, etc. Sometimes I would catch a parent signing to their child, and my parents would again steer me away. I associated signing with the "less fortunate," as my parents would always call them. My parents would always say that I was better off, did better, and would always be better and that I wasn't "like them." My high school counselor did not encourage me to look into Gallaudet, and [my] high school was located right outside of Washington, D.C.! Of course, my parents did not even mention it. Now, I REALLY wish I had been given some information about it. F 86

These stories reminded me of my experience with Mary Ellen, my childhood friend who didn't think I belonged at Gallaudet. I wonder how much of her reaction came from her sense that sign language was somehow an inferior form of communication. Participants frequently mentioned believing that sign language was "beneath them." What more powerful reason could they have for their need to dissociate themselves from other d/Deaf individuals? Interestingly, virtually all the participants who once felt this way also shared that they were later able to rid themselves of this conflicting shame by opening their minds and learning more about deafness and other d/Deaf people.

> During my solitary years, I was not entirely comfortable in meeting other deaf and hard of hearing kids, especially if they used sign language. At that time, it was the late 1970s and early 1980s, when the general public still viewed deaf and hard of hearing people as not exactly normal. And since I never really considered myself deaf, I didn't socialize with them for the fear of being labeled abnormal. Also, I didn't know sign language; usually, when deaf people see that another deaf person doesn't know sign, they don't want to get to know him. It seems to go both ways! However, when I became twelve years old, I went to visit a residential school for the deaf for the first time at my mother's suggestion. My parents wanted to scope out the school, checking its educational facilities, etc., and I wanted to see how deaf students acted at an all-deaf school. Upon arrival, I was a bit embarrassed to see so many fingers flying around! I couldn't believe that my parents would even consider putting me in this school. But after a couple hours, I started to look at deaf people differently.   F 88

In addition to their fear and mistrust of sign language, participants further felt the need to dissociate from other d/Deaf people. They were never exposed to deaf or hard of hearing adults, or they were only exposed to those who had other severe disabilities or who were employed in unskilled occupations. Most of them grew up never having met a single positive adult d/Deaf role model.

> I met some deaf and hard of hearing adults when I was younger and in the mainstream program. I was a little uncomfortable around them sometimes, the main reason being that I was quite shy about sign language. The deaf and hard of hearing adults I met often used sign language as a way to communicate. And sign language was a language I did not use at that time. While growing up, I perceived spoken English as the way to communicate. And because most people around me (including my hearing family) used spoken English, I was more comfortable with that. I felt sign language was

a language for "others." Also, some of the deaf people I met had other disabilities along with their deafness. I felt most embarrassed around them, especially when my hearing peers saw this. Some of the deaf people I met had odd jobs (i.e., factory work), and I was ashamed, thinking that deaf people were only smart enough for that kind of work. I felt I was smarter than that. M 93

How can solitary deaf and hard of hearing children surrounded by negative attitudes about d/Deaf people be expected to disclose their hearing loss? Why would they want to reveal their deafness and run the risk of being associated with such unfortunates? Are attitudes any different today? Several participants commented that the question about disclosure was the most difficult one to answer and that it brought back uncomfortable feelings. Perhaps in their hearts, they knew that the disclosure question was linked to the very core of their difficulty in maneuvering around the hearing world. They knew that they *should* disclose, but experiences where disclosure brought no remedy (or worse) disinclined them to do so.

Disclosure Begins at Home

The purpose of disclosing, presumably, is to help the hearing person(s) understand the impact of the hearing loss on interaction and to indicate that a modification of the environment, the activities, and the manner of speaking by the hearing individual(s) is needed for the deaf or hard of hearing person to be more included. Disclosure brings the invisible handicap of deafness out into the open, again presumably for some purpose. Lack of disclosure permits, enables, and perpetuates the invisibility of deafness. Lack of disclosure can stem from shame, like the proverbial "elephant in the living room." And yet more shame can result from experiences where the disclosure accomplishes nothing. *That* is something only the creation of effective solutions will change. When adults know what the solutions are and can teach these to deaf and hard of hearing children *and* their hearing peers, shame will gradually fall by the wayside.

5

Academically It Was Better Than a
Deaf School, But Socially, Well . . .

In those many conversations I had with adults who had been solitaires, perhaps the most pervasive theme was that their social lives had been discouraging, even dismal. Almost all of the books and articles I read verified as much. In their writings, project participants became conflicted trying to reconcile the advantages that their mainstream education afforded them with their less-than-optimal social experiences. Despite the difficulties they experienced during extracurricular activities, the dearth of quality friendships, the constant lack of access to everyday conversation with fellow students, and the subsequent loneliness, participants were generally satisfied with their *academic* experience, declaring, "It made me who I am."

When I saw that almost all of the participants discussed this issue, my own belief about this factor was affirmed. I received an excellent education in the Greenwich, Connecticut, public schools and at Washington College. But, as I grow older, I am continuously struck by just how much I missed as a result of my hearing loss during my K–12 and college years and the ongoing impact this has had on my life. I don't feel the loss on a daily basis, but it comes back to haunt me in ways I little expect. For example, as I revised this chapter, I realized how few specific memories I've retained from my junior high and high school years. I have already shared the most entertaining stories from my elementary school years—

the fishing, the horrible slumber party, the athletic compliments. When I try to remember my junior high years, however, I see myself walking to school alone (my neighborhood anchors Mary Ellen and Bettina went to the parochial schools in town while I went to the public schools). I see myself walking into my homeroom, feeling self-conscious. I see myself gathering up my books quickly whenever the bell rang, going directly to my next class, sitting down and getting my homework out, waiting for class to start. I never talked to anyone. I felt really uncomfortable. And it seems like this was just life as I knew it, as if this were normal for me.

Of course, junior high school is a notoriously difficult time for most of us. We all feel awkward and gawky about our bodies. And having a hearing loss and not knowing what everyone is talking about would surely contribute to a child feeling even more self-conscious and isolated. Still, I remember clearly in both junior and senior high, the other children looked like they were having a good time in the lunchroom, the hallways, the locker room, and the football games. I, on the other hand, felt I was always on the sideline of this good time.

When belaboring these social disadvantages, several Solitary Mainstream Project participants went so far as to declare that they were of such severity that no deaf or hard of hearing child should be mainstreamed alone. For them, the loneliness and lack of self-esteem resulting from the pervasive feeling of being different and left out were so damaging as to negate any academic benefits. They now feel angry and regretful about their K–12 years.

Most participants, even those who said they would choose to be mainstreamed again, conveyed some sad, if not angry, regrets. They feel that their loneliness could have been lessened if those around them had been more aware of how to help. Virtually all of the suggestions they gave for today's parents and teachers were aimed at ameliorating the pervasive social isolation apparently inherent in the solitary experience, so that today's solitaires can have a more satisfying and self-esteem-building school experience. Even those who were pleased with their mainstream educations discussed how their experience could have been improved. In writings such as the following, they anguished over what they saw as the social and emotional risks posed by the mainstream K–12 setting for today's deaf and hard of hearing children. And they recognized that reducing these risks is no easy task.

I think many things play a role in how a deaf person experiences a mainstreaming education environment. It is clear from my own experience and

My high school graduation photograph, with my hearing aid carefully concealed (it was in my right ear).

from those of other deaf kids in mainstream situations that good academics
and crappy social experiences go hand in hand. Yet, it is not always easy to
weigh the pros and cons of good academic access vs. good social access to
determine what is best for an individual deaf child or teen.   F 83

Because so many of the participants mentioned this academic posi-
tive/social negative juxtaposition in their initial writings, I asked them to
elaborate on this theme. (The exact wording of my prompt is included in
the Appendix.) I asked them to ponder how it could be possible that a
handful of participants reported that their solitary mainstream years had
been socially as well as academically positive.

By far, the most frequently mentioned factor was the quality of extracurricular activity participation. These activities, they felt, were crucial to the
development of friendships and thereby ameliorated negative social experiences. Two other factors were also frequently mentioned: interacting with
other deaf and hard of hearing children and receiving support from family
members and teachers. Factors mentioned less frequently but nevertheless
forcefully were relative ability to speak, speechread, and hear; personality;
academic ability; and the family's socioeconomic status.

The juxtaposition of positive academic experiences with poor social
experiences is almost universal to the solitary mainstream experience. My
investigations indicate that a variety of factors contribute to this quandary,
which presents a challenging situation for parents and teachers. I hope
that the exploration of these factors will prompt ideas for improving the
lot of today's solitaires.

Importance of Extracurricular Activities

Most of us know almost instinctively that extracurricular activities are
crucial to the development of deep and lasting friendships. Many adults
make their closest friends during their high school and college years
within fraternities and sororities, sports teams, or other formal and informal extracurricular activities. I have often wondered if I chose the academic field of Leisure Studies because of the early deprivation I experienced
in this area.

I can hear my friends and family members protesting, "Gina, you did
lots of fun things when you were growing up!" It's true. I grew up in an

idyllic setting where I could play outside unsupervised from an early age, roaming the streets of Cos Cob before they built the interstate. The Mill Pond was not only a stone's throw from my house, it was big enough for hours of boating in the summer and skating in the winter. After school, I would rush home, grab my skates, and, in less than ten minutes, be out on the ice. We also lived adjacent to a wooded area, and I spent many hours exploring, climbing trees, and picking wildflowers for my mother. In spite of all this fun and games, there still grew a wanting in my preteen years that just could not be satisfied.

While I engaged in certain activities with my neighborhood friends during junior and senior high school, I was not involved with any school-based extracurricular activities. I find myself wondering about the stark contrast between my excellence in physical education activities during my elementary school and junior high years and my total lack of involvement in varsity sports during my high school and college years. I can remember many times in those young years being the first picked for a kickball, soft-ball, or soccer team. Yet, during high school and college, I never played varsity sports, although I tried out for cheerleading and a team or two. To this day, I cannot really imagine any reason for my rejection other than my hearing loss. Perhaps my voice quality or discomfort with voice projection ruined my chances to be a cheerleader. It would have been nice if some-one had recognized my potential as an athlete, so I could have made a con-tribution in this area. We all need to feel valued. One of the participants spoke aptly on this subject.

> My athletic prowess won the respect of other students, and they needed me; therefore, they learned to communicate with me. Had I not participated in sports, I probably would have struggled greatly.   F 87

The ostensible purpose of extracurricular activities is to provide an avenue for the development of friendships, skills, and self-esteem. They are opportunities to prove one's value to the group, a factor especially important to a deaf or hard of hearing child. It is hardly surprising that many partici-pants mentioned these activities as greatly influencing whether they saw their solitary mainstream experiences as positive or negative.

Extracurricular activities allow time for interaction outside of the class-room. They allow peers to know you more. Excelling in something can help win friends. Unfortunately, thanks to society, peers (especially pre-teens and teenagers) seem to be "wowed" when a deaf student's talent is "surprisingly" impressive. M 93

The comment, about a deaf student's abilities being seen as "surprisingly impressive," reminds me of Mary Ellen's comment about my not belonging at Gallaudet. This participant is clearly facing the same dynamic, that his friends thought he was an exception to the rule (e.g., better than other d/Deaf people).

Extracurricular activities, by virtue of their being offered in the school setting, have been part and parcel of public education for decades. Even though many studies have shown that these activities contribute greatly to children's development and to overall social capital, financial and moral support for teachers, counselors, and coaches to guide these activities declined during the later years of the twentieth century. Such has been to the disadvantage of our society.

> The reason I am promoting involvement in extracurricular activities so much is because I think deaf students find it easier to forge friendships when they have a concrete activity base with other students. Just sitting around and talking is usually not the best way for deaf students to make friends. I want to point out that getting to know people one at a time is important, because they eventually become like a "home base." If you have a problem or are confused about something (within an activity or social situation), you can go to that person to ask for help. F 93

Thus, extracurricular activities are especially important for the solitary mainstreamed deaf or hard of hearing child because they provide a structured setting in which one can make friends. "Just sitting around and talking" doesn't work, as the above participant declared. Hearing loss makes it difficult to follow and thereby participate in conversations when conditions are not optimal. Background noise, poor lighting, fast conversation, mumbling, gum chewing, and more than one person talking simultaneously are all factors that make conversation problematic for someone relying on assistive technology and lipreading. The child will perceive voices, but they will sound like mumbo jumbo. The lunchroom, hallways, and locker rooms are rife with these unfavorable conditions. In addition to these less-than-optimal conditions, the conversations in these settings are unstructured. Students could be talking about a TV program, a teacher, another student, a love gone bad, a love discovered, a new fashion, and so on. In an extracurricular setting, however, it is more likely that the conversation will center around the activity, and thus, with the assistance of technology (e.g., hearing aids and cochlear implants) and lipreading, a deaf or hard of hearing child may find it easier to participate.

The Solitary Mainstream Project participants uniformly declared that participation in extracurricular activities gives the deaf or hard of hearing child a necessary boost for making friends with a common interest. Further, they claim that such participation enables the child to be creative and demonstrate skills in ways that might not be feasible in the academic classroom. Such participation enables the deaf or hard of hearing child to gain the respect and admiration of his or her hearing peers. Most importantly, this respect and admiration will increase the likelihood that the hearing children will modify their behavior to ease communication in unstructured settings.

> I guess the bottom line is that the hard of hearing student needs to feel like she is excelling in something other than academics. To excel in some form of social activity may compensate for any inadequacies experienced in other, more random, social circumstances. It will motivate the hearing peers to want to include the deaf child in other aspects of school life. F 87

Several respondents suggested that parents and teachers should encourage deaf children to participate in activities that are not greatly dependent on conversation, such as sports or band. Conversely, one participant discussed her own high school activity of choice (a debating club), which clearly involved a lot of talking and, as she says below, might be deemed "impossible for a mainstreamed deaf child to excel in." Her clear message to parents and teachers is to let the child choose her activities and then encourage, encourage, and encourage some more.

Parents should encourage their children to try new activities and support their efforts (no matter what the activity). For example, my primary extracurricular activities were competing with the speech team and theater, which most hearing parents might assume would be next to impossible for a mainstreamed deaf student to excel in. However, the parents should also be aware of the child's strengths and weaknesses and likes and dislikes and not allow the deafness to define what he or she can or cannot participate in. In the same vein, coaches, directors, supervisors, etc., should be just as supportive and encouraging. Never say "no" to effort. My high school speech coach could have been skeptical that I would ever succeed in speech competition. But from the very beginning, he egged me on, with great results. F 93

Some schools and communities, of course, will be able to offer a wider range of activities than others. The participants commented that a greater range would be more desirable because the child will have a greater chance of finding an activity that he enjoys. It would also increase the possibility of finding an activity led by a creative and sympathetic coach who is willing to accommodate the child in a way that perhaps takes advantage of his strengths.

I felt like a part of the band when I played the saxophone. I was not first chair, but I did enjoy making music. I participated as a cheerleader by being the mascot. I wore a heavy costume. I was seen but not heard, so my funny articulation was not an issue. F 84

High School Was Really Tough

While interaction with hearing peers was relatively easy during the elementary years, several participants commented that interaction became more difficult in middle school and high school. Although the adolescent years can be problematic for all children, they may be especially stressful for a deaf or hard of hearing youngster.

In a school environment where cliques abound and students have other things competing for their time (after-school jobs, sports, clubs, etc.), most youths do not have the maturity or desire to take the time to communicate with a deaf or hard of hearing student. I had lots of friends up until the pre-teen years (ages 10–12). At that point, the social dynamics changed. There was more verbalization, less activity. Although teachers can remind students to take turns talking or to make room for a deaf student in a group discussion, critical interaction (with no such reminders) takes place outside the classroom. Especially in middle and high school, students sitting in the back of the room whisper to each other, write notes, and talk about things other than class. Outside, they congregate at lockers, in the cafeteria (or even drive off campus), telephone each other, go away for weekends, and so forth. At this age, socialization provides about half of the education a student needs (how to relate to others, how to work in groups, learning and using various communication styles, etc.). M 87

I think that this participant's declaration that "most youths do not have the maturity or desire to take the time to communicate with a deaf or hard of hearing student" is significant. This phenomenon came to my attention again and again as this book came to life. Although hearing people, in general, do not mean harm by their actions, they frequently do not have the willingness and patience required to communicate effectively and civilly with a d/Deaf person on an ongoing basis. Why should we expect more from high school students? This pervasive lack of willingness can result in sentiments in a deaf child like those expressed below.

I didn't have friends in high school since I felt that people would be better off without me. I felt like I was a burden to others, so I felt it wise to keep a distance. This didn't seem to bother anyone—no one reached out to me. M 88

The very few Solitary Mainstream Project participants who were provided with sign language interpreters in school commented on how the presence of these adults affected social engagement. The next several excerpts show that although sign language interpreters in social and extracurricular activities may provide deaf children with information that they normally would miss, there are distinct pitfalls and inherent limitations to using them.

An interpreter is all well and good for the formal kind of classroom communication that happens, but an interpreter is an adult and an artificial third party in the communication between deaf kids and their peers in the mainstream. Deaf kids miss out on informal chatter between their class-mates because (1) the interpreter can't or doesn't want to interpret it all, and (2) because the interpreter's very presence creates a psychological barrier between a deaf student and his or her classmates that precludes the infor-mal chitchat.   F 83

Most adults will recall the great attention everyone paid to physical appearance during the high school years. This creates an extraordinary burden for the deaf or hard of hearing youngster who must contend with hearing aids, cochlear implants, and assistive listening devices, such as the infamous FM system. In general, the participants reported that they would either refuse to wear their personal hearing aids in school or use long hair to hide them, and that they particularly despised their FM sys-tems. They expressed chagrin that in addition to calling unwanted atten-tion to their "differentness," the systems had what they considered to be limited effectiveness; they enabled them to hear what their teachers were saying but not what their fellow students were saying.

As was discussed in detail in the "Best Classmates" section of chapter 3, most of the Solitary Mainstream Project participants had one or two friends who helped make their school years bearable, reiterating the point that "getting to know people, one at a time, is important, because they eventually become like a home base." It also reiterates the fact that deaf or hard of hearing children can often function effectively in a one-on-one setting, so it is helpful if they find a friend who enjoys that kind of inter-action as well. It seems logical that deaf or hard of hearing children will be befriended by someone who accepts the challenges created by hearing loss.

Parents should recognize that it's perfectly OK to spend more time one on one with a single friend than to be in small groups of friends. They should recognize that friendships with older, mature friends are perfectly OK. They model social behavior and are usually more understanding than same-age peers. Mentor programs work well in this area. Encourage "buddy" [systems] when the student doesn't seem confident with new activities and social experiences. One can influence the environment more easily in smaller, rather than larger, places. Above else, model positive and can-do attitudes and effective communication skills with the deaf student so others see that this is the best way to interact with and include the deaf student socially.   F 80

One participant relayed her mother's objections to her "clinging to one friend." It is perhaps very difficult for a parent to realize how little access deaf or hard of hearing children have to the conversations happening around them. This lack of understanding, and thereby empathy, can engender unrealistic or burdensome expectations for a solitaire's friendship circles.

> I remember my mother always being upset with me that I always clung to one friend (she wanted me to broaden my social circle). And at the time, I really didn't have the ability to communicate to her what I was going through socially. My parents' main focus was on my academics, and even to this day, when we talk about the social aspects of my childhood, they say they were completely unaware of what I was going through.   F 85

While we were discussing the social isolation I felt in my younger days, my older sister Nina commented, "Gina, you always had a friend." I think this was her way of assuring me that I had been okay, that maybe my life hadn't been so bad after all. It made me smile. I *did* have some great friends, usually one at a time. In elementary school, I was friends with Mary Ellen and Bettina (as discussed in chapter 3). Back then, I also loved exploring the backwoods, climbing trees, and doing other tomboyish things with my other friend Jeannie. We had many fun adventures together; I think of her as my first traveling companion. There were a few girls from Cos Cob School: Susan and Linda. Our friendships were short-lived but still memorable. During my junior high years, there was Eileen, a girl who lived on our street for just three years but with whom I became very close. I visited her several times annually during our teen years and during our twenties and early thirties. Diane and Sue befriended me at Central Junior High. These friendships were short-lived also, but they were memorable. At Washington College, I was friends with Kathy, Judy, and Loretta. When I was home from college during summers, there was Chris from Greenwich High and Elaine from the food store where we

My neighborhood friend Bettina and I have remained close all these years.

both worked. I made these friends before I discovered the Deaf community. I remain in touch with Chris, Kathy, and Judy in addition to my lifelong buddies Mary Ellen and Bettina.

All of these women bear mentioning because they were the only ones
willing to put in the special effort to be friends with me. They were able
to see past my hearing impairment to my more redeeming qualities. I
think it is telling that most of these girls lived on my short street (or on
my college dorm floor) and thereby were perhaps more readily accessible.
I could walk across the street or down the hall and knock on their door.
While together, we could engage in the very important one-on-one interaction that I could never achieve in a crowd or even a small group. On the

contrary, I never had this opportunity in school—there was always a crowd, large or small, and very few individuals sought me out.

These friends were and still are comfortable with how my hearing loss dictates what we can do together. For example, we can't just call each other up on the phone. When we have our rare but cherished visits, they know it would be hard for me if they threw a party or even invited a small group of friends over to meet me. On occasion, I might meet a friend of theirs, but they understand that our best quality time is when it's just the two of us.

I Needed Other Deaf Kids

Participants who were given the opportunity to interact with other deaf or hard of hearing children spoke highly of this experience. An oft-stated sentiment was illustrated in the words of one participant: "It probably wasn't until college [at Gallaudet] that I looked back and saw the extent of how isolated I truly was." Another described an imaginary ideal life where a child has both deaf and hearing friends and her parents and teachers encourage her to spend time with all of them. One participant expressed a belief that such support and encouragement would have equipped her to make better choices as an adult.

> I can envision an ideal life: Parents know sign language and are educated about Deaf culture—maybe they have a local deaf service center. They expose the deaf child to EVERYTHING: speech therapy, interpreters in school, a deaf school, and hearing aids. They take the child to special deaf social events like a bowl-a-thon, a picnic, a deaf festival, a deaf summer camp, or a National Theatre of the Deaf show. Just so that the deaf child will not be deprived of meeting others who are exactly like herself. I wish I had had this ideal life. I'd be getting a perfect balance of deaf and hearing culture. And I can guarantee that . . . trying all these choices would definitely help me later in my life to find what's comfortable for me. I would be choosing what works for me and what doesn't. And I'd be well rounded and happy.   F 91

Several mentioned that this need for deaf and hard of hearing peers was greatest in the junior and senior high school years. They also commented, however, that if a child has no contact with other deaf children during the elementary years and then is suddenly cast into their presence, he or she may reject these peers. As illustrated in chapter 4, many solitary deaf and hard of hearing children don't want to be associated with "those people."

Comments made by the Solitary Mainstream Project participants seem to suggest that contact with other deaf and hard of hearing peers ought to begin no later than the middle school years, because this is when social interaction becomes more conversation oriented and the opinions of peers take on an added importance. This next quote illustrates both the great need for affiliation at this stage of life *and* the ever-conflicting feelings deaf teens have about other deaf teens.

> When I was a child, life seemed very fast, and I cannot remember everything. All I did was play, play, and play. I had some friends who didn't notice much about my deafness. We all just played. By the time I entered the dreaded teen years, I was getting more and more confused about myself, my hearing loss, and my hearing peers. I tried so hard to be like these hearing teenagers and learn to behave like them in a hearing world way. I started to ignore my few deaf friends because I considered them inferior! Sad, huh? There was usually a lot of miscommunication between us, which always upset me. I would go home, slam the door shut, let out my frustration and anger, and then later cry. Too much pain.   M 89

Such pain motivated some participants to take on leadership roles in an effort to bring themselves into more contact with other deaf youth. In relation to the next comment, I wonder how much support this solitaire had from the school system for this activity.

> When I first met other "solitary" mainstreamed children from various local schools at a swim pool party hosted by a hard of hearing middle-aged couple, I instantly felt at home with them since we all share similar frustrations in mainstreaming. Since this couple only hosted the party once a year, I decided to get involved by planning more events. This group became known as Mainstreamed Hearing Impaired Teens.   F 86

The following excerpt illuminates the point that a deaf child may have a more active social life while attending a deaf school.

I have to admit that I received a good education in the mainstream. . . . I have always been interested in learning, reading, and just knowing things. However, my wife has pointed out that, for me, reading was in part a refuge from not having friends or a way to avoid the ostracism I experienced at the hands of others. If I had been in a school for deaf children, with normal, accessible communication, where all the other kids were like me (deaf), would I have had such a need to read? That is, assuming I would have made friends with more kids in a school for the deaf (and I think I would have, judging from my life as an adult in the Deaf community), would I have needed to seek this refuge? I have to admit, since adulthood, with more social opportunities and the advent of closed captioning, I have spent less time reading than I used to. I do feel, however, that I would have had more confidence in myself had I had more experience in the Deaf world. M 81

Comments such as the one above make one wonder which setting is more inclusive. Perhaps more importantly, it makes one wonder why we have not yet been able to provide all deaf children with the best of both educational settings in terms of academics and socialization.

Importance of Family and School Support

Participants frequently expressed the opinion that concerned adults need to learn as much as possible about what it "feels like" to be deaf or hard of hearing in a completely hearing school. When deaf or hard of hearing children have several knowledgeable and thereby sensitive adults in their environment, they will feel support and encouragement. The nature of encouragement will be shaped by an understanding of what it's like to be deaf and a solitaire, and thereby sufficiently empathic. An example of this knowledge-based encouragement would be an adult's efforts to locate and interact with other families with deaf children.

Schools need to provide more opportunities for mentors and other volunteers who can serve as role models for deaf children. The deaf kids need to meet deaf adults as well as other deaf and hard of hearing kids. There is very little exposure to other deaf children and adult role models.   F 91

Deaf or hard of hearing children will need support related to their hearing friends as well. The following is an interesting statement about how family members can help a deaf or hard of hearing child learn what topics people talk about, recognizing that he would not have access to this information simply by being in the presence of a conversation.

> Parents should talk with hearing impaired children about what people do and why they do things. What do people do and say? How should one respond to a certain situation? Discussions of those things would help the hearing impaired child gain a better insight into the hearing world. I never did have much of those types of discussions. It never occurred to me until I was an adult that this would be a helpful thing. . . . I don't believe my parents ever had an understanding or a realization of where I was coming from and how I was socializing with my peers. It was never something that would have occurred to them, given the fact that they live in a hearing world and take these things for granted.   M 85

Some readers may feel that the participants who wrote the following excerpts were given too much attention. Their parents made a point of emphasizing their uniqueness. Of course, most parents see their children as special. It seems, however, that the typical solitary mainstream social experience can be so wanting, and the harm that can be done by uninformed teachers so devastating, that a parent or other concerned adult cannot do too much damage control. It is perhaps crucial to note that these particular participants, who spoke of seemingly extraordinary attention from adults, were the selfsame handful that felt they had had an especially positive experience as solitaires. The ameliorative impact of the parents' attention cannot be overemphasized.

> I had two loving and caring parents, as well as a deaf sibling, who all accepted me for who I was and never saw my disability as a barrier, but as one of the many facets of my identity. . . . Here's the perfect story that my mother loves to tell: One day I was playing in the schoolyard, near the monkey bars that I had loved so much. It was Parent Day, and all the teachers and parents were sitting around watching the children play. I was about six years old. As always, I had my favorite outfit on, as well as the bulky hearing aid vest that I saw as my "special vest." I walked up to one of my fellow classmates, whom I will call Beth. Beth is hearing and therefore had no special vest. As we were playing, I said to her, "Your parents don't love

you!" Beth asked me, "Why not?" I said, "Because you don't have a special vest!" That story has always stuck out in my mind as how I saw myself among these normal, hearing children. My parents treated my disability as a special gift, and that carried me through all these school and college years. With that, I was able to mentally and emotionally overcome any self-doubt that my disability would have given me.   F 93

Parents can make a great difference by taking it upon themselves to alert teachers and other school-based adults to deaf children's needs. The next few excerpts describe parental actions that, while not so much focused on counteracting inevitable attacks on self-esteem, nevertheless illustrate the ample attention paid to the child's needs and actions taken to ease the way. One mother made a point to screen her child's teachers to ensure that her child would be able to lipread with relative ease.

> My mother was able to choose my teacher. The principal would ask my mother to visit the next grade up and observe all of the teachers. . . . Then, my mother would inform the principal of the teacher, in her opinion, whom I would be able to hear best. I was outfitted with one behind-the-ear hearing aid. She would pick teachers who had louder voices and spoke clearly. If my hearing aid battery died while I was at school, she would come to the school with a new battery.   F 84

Participants also mentioned the parents' ability to comfort children when they faced discouragement. One participant emphasized that his parents were always supportive of him. Although grateful for that, he acknowledges how difficult his mainstream experience was by stating, "I do not think I would do it again."

> Sometimes I would come home feeling down and upset, and my parents were quick to show me they loved and accepted me. They were good listeners. That was very encouraging to my self-esteem and was a major factor in why I do not hold as negative a view towards my mainstreaming experience. There must be a balance between the tough, "stick it out" attitude and the loving, supportive attitude displayed by parents who respond to situations their child encounters in the solitary mainstream.   M 93

These comments add credence to idea that it is critical for concerned adults to make sure that the solitary deaf or hard of hearing child has positive experiences to outweigh the negative. Life in the solitary mainstream is difficult, and a safe harbor at home can make all the difference. The trick will be learning *how* to provide that safe harbor for a deaf child.

> I think a positive solitary mainstream experience largely depends on a number of factors, the greatest of which are the self-esteem and home life of the student PRIOR to entering school. If there is good communication, a sense of belonging, and stability at home, then usually students can ride their mainstreaming experience out, whether said situation is positive, negative, or mixed. Without family interaction or support, a bad mainstreaming education is only going to be worse overall.   M 80

Ideally, both home and school would be safe harbors. Some participants believed the school should be responsible for promoting awareness and sensitivity. For them, life was unacceptably stressful, and everyone, themselves included, needed more information about how best to deal with deafness. They didn't know what they needed. They surmised that if everyone had received accurate and ample information, they would have felt better about themselves, carried themselves more confidently, and, in general, had a better school experience.

> The hearing population should learn what it is like for hearing impaired individuals to function in the hearing world and be encouraged to develop friendships with the hearing impaired. This should be done in a school setting. I don't feel it is sufficient to explain details about hearing loss itself. I think it is imperative that the hearing population be instructed on how to help the hearing impaired overcome their silent world and develop friendships.   M 85

> Acquiring sensitivity toward people with disabilities is a lifelong process, and education about it needs to be ongoing, not just limited to the seventh grade. If anything, it needs to be intensified, especially in the crucial middle and high school years, because this is when the kids really start to be mean to their peers and start ostracizing the ones who are "different."   F 94

These comments about the need to improve awareness, sensitivity, and behavior with regard to deaf and hard of hearing children suggest a pervasive lack of clarity or consensus about the respective responsibilities of parents, teachers, and school systems. This apparent ambiguity or lack of guidelines could certainly translate into negative consequences—passing the buck and finger-pointing, albeit directed by ignorance—could result in a negative experience for a deaf or hard of hearing child.

"But She Looks Like She Is Participating Just Fine!"

Adults who are unaware of the myriad factors that impact how life appears through the eyes and imperfect ears of a deaf or hard of hearing child will have a difficult time assessing the extent to which that child is having the kind of school experience that is expected for hearing children. Some of the Solitary Mainstream Project participants articulated what I have come to believe is another pervasive barrier to the improvement of life for deaf and hard of hearing children today: If activity leaders and peers are not informed about the implications of hearing loss and how to socially include the deaf or hard of hearing child, extracurricular participation will most likely be only superficial. The coaches and fellow students might think, "Oh, she is participating just fine," but the experience will be limited to just that, participation in the actual activity. The child will not be privy to the conversations that exist in and around the activity, and the coaches and fellow students will be unaware of the extent of this isolation. Imagine a soccer player in your mind's eye. She is on the field, running this way and that, and kicking the ball at appropriate times. She seems to fit in; she looks no different than the other players. But just because she can play the game doesn't mean she is hearing anything or benefiting from the inherent social interaction.

> It was great to be involved (I raced on the swim team and played lacrosse and volleyball), but with this involvement came a lot of stress. I always had a hard time hearing the coach yell the plays, hard time hearing teammates on the field, missed out on team gossip in between drills (particularly in the pool when I couldn't wear my hearing aids), would miss many of the team jokes and always dreaded the team bus rides to meets because I could never

follow all the chatter with all the noise on the bus (I would sit very quiet and feel invisible!). All that soft stuff was an important part of being or feeling part of the team.   F 85

I played on my school's winter soccer team from seventh grade to tenth grade, and neither of my coaches really understood my situation or what needed to be done to help me follow practice and encourage me to be successful at playing soccer. I enjoyed what I did; I just did not understand player meetings or feel like part of the team.   F 94

I could really relate to these comments. During all of my K–12 and Washington College years, I am quite certain that onlookers would have thought I was participating "just fine." If I wasn't actively complaining, sulking in a corner, or sitting by myself, then everything was "just fine." Clearly, when parents or teachers evaluate what it means to be "just fine," they will need to look deeper.

The next comments focus on what one participant referred to as looking "busy." He refers to an appearance of busyness (to hearing adults) as well as to a feeling of busyness within the deaf or hard of hearing child. My own life, conversations, and observations led me to believe that looking "busy" is a widespread and prevalent defense mechanism. It is part and parcel of the "he looks just fine" phenomenon.

Activities can keep deaf or hard of hearing students "busy," so that they either start to enjoy and feel a part of things (this largely depends on the reactions and communication from the other students and teachers, the type of activity, etc.), or at least keep themselves "going" and around other people so that they do not have time to feel lonely and out of place. In my secondary school years, I participated in a variety of extracurricular activities, some of which I enjoyed, and some of which kept me involved to the extent that I was "busy" and "met" people, although the social interaction was extremely limited. It probably wasn't until college that I looked back and realized how isolated I truly was.   M 87

Many deaf and hard of hearing people talk about "the dinner table syndrome." In most families, the dinner table is a place for talking and sharing. People talk about their day, their frustrations, their fun, and their purchases or contemplated purchases. To be frank, my listing of these common conversation topics are a guess on my part, based on what signing deaf people talk about over dinner and what I have seen on captioned TV! In my own family, I never was able (and still am not) able to follow dinner table conversation. This appears to be one of the most documented (in oral histories) universal experiences of deaf and hard of hearing people who are born into hearing families. My father's way of dealing with this was to busy himself with eating. By focusing on the food, he and I could look "busy" and not appear clueless as to the content of the conversation going on around us, and other family members could avoid having to deal with this uncomfortable and apparently (to them) unfixable reality.

I used this same defense technique during all of my years in mainstream cafeterias. One participant had an interesting perspective on this phenomenon. She surmised that an individual could conceivably have a positive solitary mainstream experience if she could pour herself into the academic life and just ignore the social wasteland.

> Maybe those who claim to have had a good mainstream experience either were somehow able to make friends with hearing children or they ignored hearing children altogether and concentrated solely on their studies. I think it is very possible that they may have focused solely on their studies and foregone friendship entirely.   F 81

I agree that it is possible to focus completely on an activity and ignore the conspicuous absence of socialization, because I have done this very thing myself. For several years in my adult life, I frequented a local gym, having discovered a passion for racquetball. I would arrive at the locker room with just enough time to change and run to the racquetball court. And I would leave immediately after the game, preferring to shower at home. I did this to avoid conversation. My racquetball partners probably just assumed I was too busy or unfriendly or both.

How are adults to know when a deaf child is just busying himself? Perhaps each solitary deaf or hard of hearing child needs an advocate like Claire Ramsey—someone who will observe the child often and regularly to evaluate the quality of social interaction. Most likely, superficial interaction will be prevalent. How prevalent would be too prevalent? Who needs to change, the deaf child or his hearing peers? In what ways? How can the change be instigated, and will the change take place in the reasonable near future so as to truly impact the deaf child's experience? And, who is responsible for observing the deaf child's interaction with his hearing peers? Although it may behoove parents to start thinking about these questions, the school system certainly bears responsibility as well.

Virtually all the participants suggested training activity leaders (coaches, drama and art teachers, club sponsors, etc.) and fellow students to improve the quality of extracurricular experiences for deaf and hard of hearing children. Are the deaf children responsible for educating people about their needs? Perhaps they should be involved in such training, but not responsible for it. Who is responsible for providing this training, and who should be expected to participate in such training? Is such training mandatory or optional? And, who should be responsible for evaluating the quality of the deaf children's involvement in the training? What kinds of skills would make an adult qualified to perform such an evaluation? When the solitary mainstream participants talked about the development and maintenance of such training programs, most seemed to suggest that the responsibility lies with the school system.

Teaching Others about Hearing Loss

I hope I have driven home the point that someone needs to take responsibility for educating everyone—the parents, the teachers, the classmates, and the deaf or hard of hearing children—about hearing loss and how to create the best possible solitary experience for the child. Although conceding that parents and school systems bear ample responsibility, I would like to share a bit more about what the Solitary Mainstream Project participants had to say about the children's need to advocate for themselves. A savvy and assertive child can do a lot to ease his own way. Some remarked that as the child becomes older, he will need to learn how to advocate for himself to successfully maneuver in the hearing world. Participants who advocated for themselves found the experience empowering.

> My high school health teacher encouraged me to talk with all the senior year health classes about the experience of deafness. I think it helped the other kids

understand things better, and I wish I had done that a lot earlier on in school. Some kids thought that I was stuck up when I didn't answer them but later said that my behavior made sense after hearing me talk about my communication struggles in school. Before that, they'd been puzzled. Deaf students should teach other kids to sign. That would definitely help in informal situations. It was hard for me, a naturally introverted person, to do this, but it usually paid off. I think, however, it is more the responsibility of parents and teachers to meet the deaf children's needs.   F 83

Adults involved with the lives of deaf or hard of hearing children will need to periodically ask themselves how much or what kind of advocating should be done by the parents, teachers, and the school systems. What should the deaf or hard of hearing child be expected to do? And how can the parents, teachers, and school system pave the way for the child's self-advocacy?

Relative Ability to Speak, Speechread, and Hear

The Solitary Mainstream Project participants identified a few additional factors in their ruminations about what would contribute to the quality of a child's experience. The deaf or hard of hearing children's relative ability to speak, speechread, and benefit from their residual hearing was one of these factors. I use the word "relative" because virtually all participants who mentioned this felt that a child with "better" hearing, speech, and speechreading ability would be more likely to have a positive mainstream experience. They did not really define "better" but used words such as "hard of hearing" or "moderate loss" to describe "better."

> Those who had trouble with socializing probably had a severe to profound hearing loss, whereas those who did not have trouble probably had only mild to severe hearing loss. . . . I am curious as to how any young hard of hearing person can describe a social experience as "enriching." For me, any social situation was and is hard, tedious work that requires a great deal of focus on my part. In my adult life, my job demands that I pay 110 percent attention at all meetings; and by the end of a working day, I am shot.   M 80

I found it interesting that this participant shared how he continues to experience communication with hearing peers on the job as "hard, tedious work." During my elementary years, when my hearing loss was not so profound (50 dB), I could hear most of my teachers most of the time without great effort. Following the conversation of my peers in the lunchroom, however, was impossible even with this moderate loss. Once I was in junior high school, I would describe all efforts to comprehend conversation everywhere (at school, at home, out with friends) as tasking and tiring. By then, I had a 65- to 70-dB loss. And like the participant in the next excerpt, my speech was very understandable.

> My hearing wasn't that bad. I was able to wear these annoying hearing aids; but still, they're good to use. My voice is perfect, and I can speak "fluent" English, and you cannot notice if I am deaf or not. So, that caused my parents to think that I was okay when I was not okay. Big mistake.   M 89

Thus, speaking well can have its downside. It can contribute to the "But he looks like he is participating just fine" syndrome. If a child has good speech and perhaps a moderate hearing loss, she may appear to understand all or most information when, in fact, she does not. This is yet another area in which parents and teachers can take a deeper look.

Personality

Personality was mentioned by more than a handful of the participants as a factor that could contribute to a solitary child's success in the school environment. A very outgoing, "bubbly" personality would help the child succeed, and a very quiet, introverted personality would be a liability. Several participants commented that although they thought of themselves as outgoing and presented themselves to their world as outgoing, deep inside, they were insecure and full of struggle in their private moments.

> I think a child's ability to be successful in the solitary mainstream largely depends on his personality traits and how he copes with his impairment. I for one was a very happy and joyful child on the outside, even though inside I felt like I didn't belong at times. I did my hardest to smile and laugh with others, even though I didn't hear them. I really pushed myself to be very positive in everything I did. I never shared any of the negative aspects of my hearing loss with my friends or let them see that I thought I was handicapped. I believe that played a big difference in how I was perceived

by my peers. They saw that I was a positive youth and didn't let my impairment control me. Everyone wants to be around positive people. However, even though I was good at internalizing my feelings of sadness and worthlessness inside during the day, I remember many times at night crying it out at home in private where no one could see me. It was tough for me, I'm still like this, and I am such a strong person in public, even to this day.   F 91

Academic Ability and Socioeconomic Status

A few participants noted that a child's better-than-average academic ability could bring recognition and peer admiration, and that such would help balance the negative effects of social isolation. I know that this was true for me. My one area of positive self-esteem has always been in the academic area. It seems natural that I would find myself still to this day immersed in this environment.

A few also mentioned socioeconomic status, conceding that this can affect any child, a deaf or hard of hearing child no less.

Summary

A majority of the Solitary Mainstream Project participants felt that they had the best academic experience possible, considering their hearing loss and other available educational placements. On the other hand, a great majority also said that their academic experience was exceptionally better than their social experience.

Because this juxtaposition was the most common theme in the initial essays, I asked the participants to elaborate and tell me what factors they thought contributed to it. In response, they mentioned several important factors: participation in extracurricular activities; contact with other deaf and hard of hearing children; family and school support; relative ability to speak, lipread, and use residual hearing; and personality.

Unfortunately, concerned parents frequently become involved in lengthy legal and bureaucratic procedures when they attempt to advocate for their deaf child's needs. A child is only a child for a short period of time, and when remedial actions are stonewalled, the child suffers. In no time, he will move on to the next grade, and the next, and the next. As the following participant states, deaf or hard of hearing children may complete their entire school career before effective change can take place.

> I think each student needs to be viewed individually prior to placement. Some students can handle being in the mainstream; others cannot. The student needs to be listened to at all times. If it seems that mainstreaming isn't working, then residential schools or other alternatives need to be looked into. The student has one shot at an educational experience during a crucial stage in life. You can't make up for that later.   M 87

In my introduction, I mentioned the stance that many deaf scholars have taken with regards to inclusion. I found it heartening that so many of the Solitary Mainstream Project participants recognized the importance of extracurricular activities *and* exposure to other deaf and hard of hearing children and adults. In chapter 9, I will provide suggestions on how we might ensure that these needs are met—so that the solitaires of today and tomorrow will no longer feel so alone.

6

Social Life in Adulthood:
The Oasis

I HAVE often marveled at how, in spite of obvious or subtle messages from family and society to the contrary, numerous solitaires decide in adulthood that they have a good deal to gain from association with other deaf and hard of hearing people and with hearing people who use sign language. They see that their lives are greatly enriched by involvement in clubs, sports groups, monthly dinner get-togethers, and many leisure activities where communication and understanding are relatively easy because everyone uses a visual language. They are excited, gratified, and often relieved to be involved with signing deaf, hard of hearing, and hearing persons, because there is no need to constantly explain their hearing loss, constantly strain to lipread, or constantly worry about access issues. They have found their "oasis," so to speak. In an address to the 1877 meeting of the Empire State Association of the deaf, Henry Rider, a leader of New York's nineteenth-century Deaf community, gave the following reason for deaf people's frequent gatherings: "[They are], to us, what the oases of the great Desert are to famishing travelers."[1]

When I first arrived at Gallaudet at the age of twenty and discovered that I did not always have to make a huge effort to follow conversations, I couldn't see how I could ever return to my "old life" as a "hard of hearing person in a hearing world." For as long as I could remember, I had simply hated that aspect of my life. I hated not being able to participate in group conversations. I hated that my friendships depended so much on others' ability to speak clearly enough that I could lipread them. My friends, bless their hearts, were wonderful. They were the best friends I could have had, considering the circumstances. When I was growing up, however, I wished I could participate fully in a wider variety of social activities with these friends as well as with more acquaintances. Instead, my satisfying interactions with friends were limited to one-on-one conversations in our respective homes or college dorm rooms. I wanted more casual friends but basically I had none. If a fellow student didn't know me really well from lots of one-on-one conversations, he or she didn't know me at all.

At Gallaudet, I began the long process of fitting myself into the deaf world and refitting myself into the "hearing world" beyond Gallaudet's boundaries. I had lived in that the hearing world all my life, but was not satisfied with how I fit. I wanted a better, new way of fitting. This process of finding my place in the deaf world and readjusting to the hearing world has lasted for thirty years so far. When the first germinations of this book were sprouting in the Gallaudet bookstore and library, I realized that I had gone through a number of transitions since arriving at Gallaudet. I had gone from viewing myself as a hard of hearing person in a hearing world to viewing myself as a deaf person who grew up in the solitary mainstream, who now chooses how much time to spend with signers and how much time to spend with nonsigners. Over the years, I have moved through several communities in which a good number of deaf, hard of hearing, and hearing people use sign language as well as spoken language. I have also been involved with some hearing communities where I have been "the only one." In those communities, my deafness and the resulting communication issues always play a role in defining where and how I fit.

I have also met deaf and hard of hearing people who have chosen to remain as solitaires. They seem to prefer maintaining their status as the only deaf or hard of hearing person in their world. They claim to see no benefit in learning sign language or associating with other deaf or hard of hearing people. Sometimes they might have one or two oral deaf friends but for the most part they have chosen to spend their leisure time as adults predominantly or exclusively with hearing people.[2] Although I cannot fathom such a choice for myself, I feel an affinity with it because my father lived that way for the duration of his life. He continued with that choice for twenty-five years beyond my arrival at Gallaudet, despite my efforts to reform him. He apparently never recognized the benefits that sign language would have brought to him and our family. He had not the slightest motivation to learn sign.

One year, I treated my parents to a weeklong summer class in beginning sign language on the Gallaudet campus. My mother was reasonably interested and willing, but my father seemed uncomfortable and kept saying, "I just want to go to the museums." He claimed that he was too old to learn; he was in his mid-fifties at the time.

Planning To Be Included

Thus far, I have shared bits and pieces of my own journey, my evolution from the only hard of hearing kid in school to an active member of the Deaf community. Today, it is possible for me to see that a number of threads in my current life are directly connected to my beginnings as a solitaire. I think that the social deprivation I experienced during those years shaped my entire professional career. The bulk of my endeavors has been in the area of extracurricular activities, though their adult counterparts are called recreational or leisure activities.

When I turned thirty, I began to realize that this organizing had always been a major theme in my life. Not withstanding my hearing loss, I was a planner of activities during all my years in the solitary mainstream. During my elementary school years, my yard was one of several impromptu playgrounds for the neighborhood kids. Our house was in the middle of a half-acre, which contained stone walls and trees that made great props for the many games I invented using these natural hiding places and home bases.

Later, while in junior high school, I would plan for my friends and me to go downtown to hang out on Greenwich Avenue almost every weekend. On weekends during high school, I would always take the lead in getting us to go to one of the teen dances that were regularly held around town. I realize now that this was my way of controlling things so I would be included.

It is easy to see why I took the lead in planning games and organizing social activities. As I discussed earlier, sometimes my neighborhood rival would convince my two friends not to play with me. I would find myself at home alone on a Saturday. My mother or my sister would ask "Where are your friends?" and for some reason I was embarrassed that I had been ostracized. The pain of being left out was exacerbated by my knowledge that "everyone else" knew that I had been left out, and therefore would think I was an undesirable person. This pain, I believe, led me to develop a specific coping mechanism: I began to plan activities. During my teen years, all the churches and community centers in my town and the surrounding area would have regular dances. These places had names like the Rendezvous and the Haven. I would always be the first to call my friends and say, "Let's go to the Rendezvous this Friday. My sister can pick us up if your Dad or Mom can drop us off." Taking the initiative to organize an activity was a way of coping with my fear of being left out——it guaranteed that I would be included.

The dances we attended were really loud, and people didn't talk to each other much. They just stood around, watched each other dance, and hoped to be asked to dance. Not only did I not have to worry about seeming odd if I was not involved in a conversation, but I was very confident of my dancing skills. This made it easier for me to go to these dances throughout my high school years.

When it came time for college, I chose a small, rural, liberal arts institution. There my existence became very subdued. I studied significantly more than the other students, worked in the library, and participated in intramural sports. I tried to do things that didn't involve too much conversation. I went on some dates, and to this day, I marvel at how I could so diligently avoid ever saying anything. I wonder what my dates thought of me. One of these days, I will get up the nerve to go to a reunion and find out. After three years at Washington College, I felt that only a tiny handful of students really knew me. I felt isolated, even in that idyllic setting with only 650 fellow students.

People ask me why I chose Washington College. It was very small and in a very remote rural area, and many people had never heard of it. When

I was in the ninth grade, my government class took a trip to Washington, D.C. Whether it was the beauty of the monuments amid the cherry blossoms or the fact that it was my first trip anywhere without my family, I fell in love with the landscape and the idea of "The Nation's Capitol." So, when as a high school senior, I sat in the guidance counselor's office looking through the college catalogues, I noticed "Washington College" and assumed it was in Washington, D.C. I soon learned it was not actually in Washington, D.C., but ninety minutes away.

After spending my senior year at Gallaudet, I was grounded in that place. Here, friends from Gallaudet help me give my fellow Washington College classmates best wishes for our college yearbook.

During the summers of my college years, I would go back to Cos Cob and organize trips to bars with any one of my one-on-one friends who happened to be available. I never stayed home on a weekend night. These outings were more socially difficult for me because not every bar had a dance floor for me to escape to. Many times, people would just stand around and talk. So I would simply stand there and never say anything. Still, it was better than staying home and facing the painful awareness of being left out.

By this time, I was very aware that my access to conversation in most environments was sorely limited. As a result, I became disheartened about the prospects for my future. I was loath to think that my life would always be like that, that I would never be able to participate in group discussions or even in one-on-one conversations unless the conditions were just right. I felt that my hearing loss presented a huge limitation for both my personal life and my career options.

For a long time, I had wanted to be a psychologist, and one day it dawned on me that this was a ridiculous goal for someone like me. I could just see myself with a patient lying on a couch, explaining her problems to me. Deep, serious, distressing problems. And I would ask, "What did you say? Please say that again." Not only would I have to ask them to repeat things, I would have to incessantly ask them to repeat things. I knew this would be the case because I had met many people who were really hard to lipread even in quiet environments. It didn't seem like it would be a very therapeutic experience for the patient!

I caught a glimpse of a different kind of life, however, on that serendipitous day in the Washington College cafeteria when I first laid eyes on those Gallaudet soccer players having their animated conversation That day, I realized that there was a whole group of people who communicated using sign language, and a desire to be with them began to grow in my heart.

During my sophomore year, I took a class called "Introduction to Education," and in this class I had my first opportunity to learn more about other d/Deaf people other than the fact that they existed. One of the course requirements was to teach the subject of our choice at the local elementary school. I shyly asked Dr. McHugh if he thought it would be a good idea for me to teach the kids about deaf people. To my pleasant surprise, he thought it was a wonderful idea. With this encouragement, I began studying books about deaf people (not that there were many in 1969). I recall adding some fun to my lesson plan by teaching the children a joke in sign language. So, my first lesson in sign language was self-taught. This assignment was my first attempt to teach hearing people about deafness, an important experience that many of the Solitary Mainstream Project participants mentioned.

As I thought about my future career, I figured I could be a psychologist for deaf people. To attain this goal, I realized I needed to learn a lot more sign language, and the best place to learn sign would be Gallaudet College in Washington, D.C.

Emboldened by Dr. McHugh's support, I approached the chair of the psychology department, Dr. Kirkpatrick, and asked if I might spend my senior year at Gallaudet College. With his support and that of the dean, Dr. Seeger, my career was launched.

My parents brought me to Gallaudet in August 1971, a special time for me. I took classes that were electives to me, having completed all the courses for my major at Washington College. English, philosophy, public speaking, and badminton—I thought I had died and gone to Liberal Arts Heaven.

Not only were the subjects varied and interesting, but the coursework was easy for me, being a senior with three years of rigorous academics under my belt. Most days, I would finish any homework by 8 p.m. and go to the Rathskellar, Gallaudet's popular pub. There I would sit until closing time, talking, listening, and watching conversations and people rendering popular music into sign language. Many Gallaudet students had hearing aids and could enjoy music. So, I was in Group Conversations Heaven as well!

When time came to graduate, returning to Washington College for commencement was a very mixed bag for me. I was pleased that my entire family came down for the festivities. I felt lots of pride as I looked into the eyes of Drs. McHugh, Kirkpatrick, and Seeger—those who had encouraged and made possible my memorable year at Gallaudet. But I realize now I was confused about who I was. Was I a Washington College student, or was I a Gallaudet student? In which world did I belong? For a long time to come, I would feel that I was straddled on a fence between the Deaf world and the hearing world.

After the Washington College commencement, I returned to Washington, D.C., to work at Gallaudet. I felt sadness at having to choose between the two worlds, but no Deaf people lived in Greenwich. And after spending ten months in their midst while studying at Gallaudet, I knew that I could not live without these people—my people. During that first year at Gallaudet, I told my mother, "Mom, after graduation I am coming back home." But, shortly before graduation, I had to tell her, "Mom, I'm sorry, but I'm not coming back home."

When I embarked upon the Solitary Mainstream Project, I knew that this sense of belonging with other d/Deaf people was something many of us had discovered along the way. In fact, a majority of the participants mentioned this in their responses to my open-ended invitation to tell me anything significant about their school years. The code word (within the data analysis software program I was using) I selected to identify the writing segments that focused on this was "metdeafwow." I thought this captured the sense of excitement relayed. I asked them to elaborate on this with the following prompt:

> More than half of you mentioned that you were thrilled to meet other deaf or hard of hearing children or adults in your K–12 or college years and wish you had met them earlier in your life. At the same time, many of you mentioned being "afraid of" or "uncomfortable around" other deaf and hard of hearing children and adults when you were younger. Talk about this with regard to yourself. In particular, try to explain why you were "uncomfortable" or "thrilled" to meet other deaf and hard of hearing children.

"Metdeafwow": No More Shame

As we saw in earlier chapters, many of the participants internalized a belief during their K–12 years that other deaf or hard of hearing people were lacking or abnormal. A great majority, however, later changed to accept and even embrace other deaf and hard of hearing people. In writings like the one below, they described how contact with others who were like themselves had a very positive impact on their lives.

> Even so . . . if I had met them in my younger years, I am sure that the dis-comfort would have quickly gone away and I would have learned more about myself and being deaf. I missed out on that opportunity. I did even-tually meet other deaf people my age when I became twelve or thirteen. I attended a camp for deaf children. This was not only my first time away from home but also my first exposure to living with deaf people. I ate, slept, and breathed with deaf people 24/7, and it was a good experience for me. I became more open and understanding and accepting of my deafness from then on. I enjoyed learning sign language; I enjoyed being able to partici-pate fully in conversations, whereas with hearing children, I was always left out. That camp was a turning point for me, and today, 18 years later, I am still involved with that camp!   F 87

The next excerpt was written by a participant who, like me and several others who made presentations to hearing classmates, came to know about the Deaf community via personal research. This participant's early career direction paved the way for her to find "somewhere [she] belonged."

> As I began to come out of my shell, I ordered books from Gallaudet Uni-versity Press. I must have ordered twenty-five or so books and read them that summer before starting my master's program. It was through these books that I began to understand that there was a culture. . . . And, that I was not alone. While I was in grad school, I decided to do my master's the-sis on some aspect of deafness. From there, I had to gather "subjects" for my study, and this is when I really began to get into contact with other deaf people. From there on, I began to socialize with other deaf people. I found a few with whom I felt comfortable and realized that I had found some-where I belonged.   F 84

Much of what the participants shared in response to this prompt was similar to their comments relayed in chapter 5, where they expressed their need for greater contact with deaf and hard of hearing peers. It is impor-tant to emphasize that statements about this need were interspersed with statements about their concomitant difficulty feeling comfortable around other deaf and hard of hearing people.

> When my parents first took me to visit our state deaf school, I really did not want to be there. I just wanted to leave. After about a couple hours though, I started to look at deaf people differently. I wanted to communicate with them as fluently as they could with each other, because I started to feel like I belonged. Where was my easy communication with the hearing people? Here, I would never miss out on what the teacher said. I would be on the same social level, play sports, learn to be more assertive, and on and on. But, it wasn't until I was transferred to a mainstreamed program at the age of 16 [I never did attend that deaf school] that I socialized with deaf and hard of hearing peers more than with hearing peers. By that time, I was more comfortable being around them than I was during my younger years. It took a while for me to accept myself as one of them.   F 87

So because I wanted to be "one of them," I returned to Gallaudet immediately after graduation. My first job was as administrator in charge of student activities, planning cultural events, coffeehouse nights, and various festivals. My experience planning junior and senior high school social activities finally paid off professionally! Following eight years of this, I was itching to move on to something more challenging. The logical career step would have been to move to a similar job at a larger university; however, I was loath to leave Gallaudet for any reason. I had not yet had my fill of "metdeafwow" activities. I couldn't stand the idea of returning to the hearing world on a nine-to-five basis.

To satisfy my restlessness for something new, I made some lateral moves within Gallaudet. The first of several jobs in a five-year period was in the President's office, where I learned about P.L. 94-142. While thusly confined to business attire and a nine-to-five routine, I also embarked on my professional fitness career.

When I turned thirty, I became an exercise fanatic. This obsession has held me in good stead, as I can say I have exercised faithfully four to six times per week for the past twenty-three years! Not many people can say that. This appears to be the first of several life excursions back into the solitary mainstream on a part-time basis in the leisure arena. In all of these excursions, I invited my deaf and hard of hearing peers to join me. I wanted to participate in hearing world activities, but I wanted signers, deaf or hearing, alongside me.

I started my exercise career with jogging. Jogging was new, and I liked it. It made me feel good. I had this idea that I wanted to live to be one hundred and thought jogging would certainly increase my chances of doing so. Shortly after I began jogging, I noticed a new building being built in my neighborhood with a sign that proclaimed it was the "Future Home of the Laurel Racquetball Club." I wanted to add other exercise activities to my boring jogging routine, and here was a place to do that. So join I did. Numerous weekend tournaments kept me busy for a while, but it didn't take me long to start missing my d/Deaf friends and the socializing that would go along with the activity if they were there with me. So, I started organizing Deaf racquetball tournaments at my club. Soon I had regular d/Deaf partners, both male and female, and was participating in Deaf tournaments around the country.

One day, I saw an advertisement in my local newspaper: "Aerobic Dance Classes: Oaklands Elementary School, Tues/Thurs 7–8 p.m." I decided to give that a try as well. After several months, I again decided that participating with hearing people was just not satisfying enough and embarked upon efforts to become an instructor so that I could bring this activity to the Deaf community. Within two years, I had achieved this goal and went on not only to instruct exercise classes for the next fifteen years but to become a recognized leader in the greater fitness world as well.

When hearing people join a racquetball club or an exercise class, they give hardly any thought to the other people who will be attending. They fully expect to meet people, talk with them, and perhaps find a new friend. In fact, when people actually want new friends, they tend to join recreational activities because they'll meet other people who share similar interests. For d/Deaf people, however, membership at the racquetball club and participation in the neighborhood aerobic dance classes are usually not socially productive. For the Women's Tuesday Night Ladder (a program where you challenge the person just above you on a list), I would show up just in time to play, and then leave as soon as my game was over. I would even shower at home because I did not enjoy being in the locker room—people would chitchat, and I would end up feeling left out and alone, similar to how I felt during my solitary mainstream days. Working at Gallaudet, I rarely, if ever, felt that way, and I didn't like dealing with it again. I now understood well the difference between conversations where I would strain to hear, pretend to hear, or simply bow out, and the wonderful conversations that I could and would have with other signers. I most definitely preferred the latter. I didn't like that anxious feeling I got from trying and failing to access conversations with people who did not sign. I didn't like having to stop an interesting conversation in order to explain my hearing loss.

I spent my thirties and half of my forties organizing racquetball tournaments and aerobics classes. It was as if I was finally expressing my long-dormant athletic ability as well. My natural organizing skills only added to my success in establishing settings where I could exercise my athletic ability while in the company of people using sign language.

Further, it is interesting to compare my motivations for planning activities during these years with those that fueled my childhood and teen organizing. During the latter, my actions were prompted by my fears of being left out. During my adult years, however, I discovered leisure activities that I truly enjoyed and wanted to share these activities in socially comfortable settings. To my deaf and hard of hearing friends, I was saying, "Hey! Here is a fun activity they do out in that hearing world. But it's no fun alone! So, join me!" I was rejecting the old solitary mainstream and molding my environment to my liking.

Choosing To Be Part of Two Worlds

Today, I am a faculty member in the Department of Physical Education and Recreation at Gallaudet University. My lifelong involvement in organizing leisure activities and my evolving professional understanding of the role leisure plays in our individual and collective life satisfaction has led me to conclude that most deaf and hard of hearing adults, if given a viable choice, will not choose to remain in the solitary mainstream for the bulk of their lives. If given a viable choice, most will do what I have done, and what most of the solitary mainstream participants have done—organize their lives to include the best of what both the hearing and Deaf worlds have to offer.

By viable choice I mean a choice based on the belief that the hearing social world and the Deaf social world are equals. This belief needs to be held in both the hearing and Deaf worlds and should be communicated overtly and covertly throughout popular culture. To say that is like saying that the social lives of black Americans with their cultural values is equally as satisfying as the social lives of white Americans. Or it is like saying that the social life revolving around a small Southern Baptist church is as acceptable as that revolving around a New England pub, like the one in *Cheers*. If the hearing culture conveyed the message that sign language use by adults is perfectly fine then such a viable choice could be facilitated. For those who grow up in the solitary mainstream, such a message would truly enable them to freely consider their options—continuing as solitaires in the hearing world or embarking upon a lifestyle that includes other deaf and hard of hearing individuals and sign language.

I was struck by how often the sixty participants of the Solitary Mainstream Project mentioned their sense of elation when first realizing there were other children in the world like themselves. I knew that my story would not be complete without discussing my transition from the hearing world to the Deaf world. Although my transition began in college, other solitaires begin theirs in high school or adulthood. And some (like my father and grandfather) never make the transition. Maybe someday I will have the good fortune to learn more about these ancestors of mine. It would give me great joy to learn that some of them belonged to a vibrant Deaf community.

That more than 80 percent of the study participants chose to learn sign language, befriend at least a few other deaf and hard of hearing individuals, and craft a social life that includes these friends, speaks volumes. It demonstrates that, despite centuries of effort to persuade the world that deaf people ought not fraternize with each other, despite intent or happenstance to expose them only to hearing peers, despite efforts to convince them that inclusion is best for them, a majority chose, as adults, to be part of the Deaf world.

Why? Because it's easier. And because satisfactory leisure time, which greatly contributes to overall life satisfaction, of necessity includes satisfactory involvement in conversation.

Recently, I had the good fortune to work with a young graduate student. Although not a complete solitaire (he had attended an oral mainstream program for part of his K–12 years), he had chosen to be a solitaire during his college years. His first professional job in a private firm propelled him toward the Deaf community. His following comments about being a solitaire remain deeply embedded in my mind.

> When I worked for that company, there was sort of a café that people from various companies would go to for lunch. I thought I would have to eat by myself because everyone seemed to be afraid to talk to me. But this one guy, he was kind of cool. He was friendly and talked to me, and we had lunch together a few times. He was easy to lipread, and so lunch was fun. But then he started telling other people they should join us. . . . I guess he wanted other people to meet me too. . . . But once there were more people, they would just all talk and talk and talk, and I didn't understand anything. . . . So after a few times, I stopped going there and would just go off by myself for lunch. (personal communication, 2002)

Many people, including this young man's former coworkers, will respond to this little story by protesting that he should have informed his coworkers of his difficulty participating in conversation so that they could have made more of an effort to include him. But what would these efforts be and how effective would they be in facilitating the d/Deaf person's participation? And at what cost to the hearing coworkers' sense of an easygoing, enjoyable lunch break? My experience in more than twenty years of forays back into the mainstream tells me that any solution short of having all the parties involved learn sign language is just too hard on everyone and thereby does not become a satisfying long-term solution.

So, because of my great interest and hunches in this area, I asked the participants to further elaborate with the following prompt:

How do you spend your leisure/social time? Describe your leisure/social involvement with other deaf and hard of hearing persons (spouse, friends, children, whatever). Also, describe your leisure/social involvement with hearing adults and/or children. Mention leisure/social time spent alone if you feel that is significant. Finally, tell me if you are satisfied with your current leisure/social life. If not, what changes would you like to see?

Analysis of the responses to this question revealed that only eight of the sixty participants in the Solitary Mainstream Project have chosen to remain fully in the hearing world. They do not know sign language, have no d/Deaf friends, and express little inclination to change this fact.

I Spend All My Leisure Time with Hearing People

Let me first introduce you to a young woman I will call Jane. She is a doctoral student at a large university and has chosen to remain pretty much the only deaf individual in her world. Although she has had ample opportunity to do so, she has never visited a nearby university where a large number of deaf students are in attendance. Jane did, however, meet other oral deaf people during the years prior to her high school graduation in 1994.[2] Her experiences with them have been less than satisfactory. She laments the fact that she has yet to meet another oral deaf person with whom she can relate by virtue of common interests and goals. Those she has met, she found to be "self-centered and high school-ish." In addition, she expresses disappointment with some young oral deaf college graduates who she sees as "lacking ambition" and "mired in depression and setbacks . . . becoming 'typical' low-functioning deaf persons." In the following, she writes about her current social life as a graduate student.

> Today, I spend my leisure time with mostly hearing people. I socialize with my oral deaf and hard of hearing counterparts at the [national] conventions (as best as I can) and keep up a correspondence over e-mail with two people. But it is mostly with my hearing peers that I hang out, doing the usual social things and the usual cultural excursions. My best friend of five years currently lives fifteen minutes away from me. We met as undergraduates and see each other about once a month, sometimes more, and talk on the phone (via relay) regularly.

During the school year, my social life centers on the weekly social hour at the [certain club] lounge and the Friday night dinner at the [other club], both of which involve a great deal of singing, participation, and some socializing. I look forward to my Friday nights with the undergrads. Most are undergrads, though there are a few grad students. But I am young enough to remember my college days and am able to hang out with the college kids, because they are my break from the usual grad school grind. I would say I am pretty much satisfied with my current leisure/social life. F 94

Jane wishes her relationships with hearing peers were more satisfying. "I do wish that my hearing friends would initiate more relay calls, would return my calls, and would invite me out a little more to do things," she says.

Jane also chooses to spend ample time alone, taking advantages of the many cultural opportunities in her urban neighborhood. One could surmise that she conducts her life like any highly intellectual young academic, minus stimulating group debates on various philosophical topics. This is a young woman who has taken a straight path from the baccalaureate to the doctoral degree. Her parents have clearly instilled in her a strong work ethic. She now has a cochlear implant and reports that she enjoys the process of "re-learning to hear."

Another participant, whom I will call Alice, is six years older than Jane and also grew up in an urban area. She does not recall meeting any deaf or hard of hearing children during her K–12 years but met several during her college years. She explains in some detail that relations with these other deaf students were strained for disparate reasons. In one case, Alice explained, the individual "spoke well" but "was a poor lipreader even though he had more hearing than me. . . . I was uncomfortable in having to repeat what I said to him [even though] my speech was audible and clear enough." Another individual was "fluent in signing ASL and speaking English," but Alice felt that their conversations were unacceptably influenced by that young woman's self-centered nature. A third individual turned out to have a "different personality and was a smoker," and thus, Alice says, they "did not get along." Finally, when in her mid-twenties, Alice met a deaf person who would become a close friend.

We've had some great one-on-one times together on our job and outside of our work hours. We were thrilled to meet each other since we mingled real well together. We have the same philosophy about life, similar family backgrounds, schooling experience, and similar opinions. And our senses of humor clicks right on between us. We seldom talk about our hearing impairment problems. This person is one of my closest girlfriends (the only one who is hearing impaired), and I keep in touch with her by e-mail usually once a month, and we often go out at least four times a year. F 80

Alice and Jane's writings show the possible role of pure serendipity. For several participants, not being in touch with other deaf or hard of hearing people may not be a conscious choice. Rather, they have simply never had the opportunity to meet another deaf or hard of hearing person with whom they could relate. Perhaps as they become older, they will have more opportunities to meet others like themselves. Perhaps they will make an effort to meet other deaf and hard of hearing people who share their interests and values.

The following are excerpts from two single males that demonstrate how other personal characteristics or circumstances (where they choose to live, the kinds of jobs they have, whether or not they have children, desire for friends of similar religion, values, etc.) affect the availability of social opportunities for each of these individuals. Each has clearly made the best of the particular opportunities and limitations of their particular corner of the world. Although they are relatively satisfied, they express some frustrations with communication challenges.

Since graduating from high school and attending college, my social experiences have been largely with hearing individuals. I go to church with hearing people. Several friends and I have gone fishing over the past few years; we just enjoy getting away from the city and getting into the scenic mountains of [state]. My social experiences are generally limited to one-to-one interactions. Group situations are too much for me. I do attend a men's [religious] group, and the members of the group have been helpful in ensuring that I am able to follow their conversations. If the conversations shift to a different person, the other group members have helped me to identify the current speaker quickly. They have also helped in slowing down, and I am very appreciative of what they have done to make me a part of the group. This experience has been the exception to the norm. Often, people are not willing to make the extra effort.

Meanwhile, my contact with the hearing impaired population has been very limited. [d/Deaf people from my state] either have given up or hide in the woodwork, or they live out of state where they have more support and understanding. I did attempt to join a support group for the hearing impaired but found the experience highly unsatisfactory. Communication was extremely difficult because I am oral, and most members of the group signed. There were several who were oral; but I didn't want to pursue friendships with them because their philosophies were different from mine. I am a conservative, religious person, and it was hard to establish friendships with those having different outlooks.

Generally, I am satisfied with my current social life, although some things could be better. I do poorly in group situations and sometimes find people migrating towards others who are hearing, because it isn't easy for them to communicate with me. There have also been many occasions when I wish I had satisfying friendships with people in the hearing impaired community.   M 85

The next excerpt is from a man who lives in a suburban town, and his location has made a difference in how he "solved his problem" in his particular environment.

My job requires that I attend many social functions with clients. Attending these functions is important to my success. However, it is not something that I do for enjoyment. I lipread very well, and in some of these situations, I can manage. But it is very hard work, and I need to take many breaks during the course of the event.

Although I have had my problems with socializing, I have solved the problem by becoming actively involved in my community by working with the church and two other local hearing organizations. If a social event requires that I do something physical, such as cooking pizza frita at a booth during a festival or a church fundraiser or simply cleaning up, I tend to enjoy it more than if I was just a visitor to the event. I find that a combination of doing something physical within a social event, such as putting up a tent for a church event, is the most enjoyable and satisfying way for me to socialize, and you have something to show for your good time as well.   M 80

A Few Deaf Friends

Thirteen of the Solitary Mainstream Project participants report themselves to be primarily oral but have some limited contact with deaf and hard of hearing adults as well. Although in a few cases, this limited contact is with other oral deaf adults, most of these thirteen know the basics of sign language, use it in their contact with their d/Deaf friends, and express a wish for more friends who sign. In addition, some of them have met other deaf adults through the Internet.

Although they report their involvement with d/Deaf people to be limited, it appears to be a source of considerable support. A representative excerpt is from a woman whose husband and friends are almost exclusively hearing. But, she has become very involved with deaf and hard of hearing organizations, has established a consulting business related to sign language, and keeps in touch with a few "deaf soul mates" via e-mail. Thus, she meets her need for involvement with the Deaf community while remaining primarily a solitaire in the mainstream.

> I am a member of [deaf and hard of hearing organizations]. I am a board member of an organization for the hearing impaired. As part of my consulting firm, I offer baby sign and basic sign language classes. I am also affiliated with a special mentoring program that Big Brothers/Big Sisters is doing for children who have hearing loss. Socially, I have a few deaf soul mates with whom I keep in contact via e-mail. Every now and then, we'll whip out the TTY and have a live conversation back and forth, but e-mail is how I keep in touch. We serve as a support group for one another for when times are good and for when we are struggling in our respective careers. Most of my day, however, is spent in the hearing world. I am married to a hearing man; all of my family is hearing; and I teach college classes at a hearing college. I work with hearing police departments in my consulting firm. Every now and then, a hearing impaired person may call wanting information, resources, or a consultation, and I take those calls. My

husband and I "married" my family since they live closely. All of the family gatherings are hearing oriented. Every now and then, the organization for the hearing impaired that I'm involved with has a social function, and my husband and I will attend. He knows that I need this outlet.

We have a "communication-friendly" house that is geared for hearing loss. My husband found me a cellular phone that is compatible with my behind-the-ear hearing aid. He likes me to go to the movies with him and always asks for assistive listening devices. But, for me, I would rather curl up on the couch with him and watch a captioned video. Also, my husband has started to sign more. What would I change? I guess I'd want his signing to improve to include more vocabulary and for him to use it more frequently.   F 84

These thirteen solitaires, who report themselves to be "oral but know some signs," engage in concerted efforts to find and maintain a few deaf or hard of hearing friends and express an interest in learning more sign language. The last excerpt from this group illustrates that most of these oral individuals, while still functioning primarily in environments like those of their K–12 (and college) years, have a need and desire to share common experiences for their mutual benefit.

I never had any deaf or hard of hearing friends, so I can't comment on my leisure/social involvement with them. However, an audiologist recently introduced me to another female my age with the same hearing impairment as me. We were both looking to make a friend with a hearing impairment, so the audiologist got us together through e-mail. Me and my friend have been e-mailing each other for the past two weeks, and it's been really wonderful. We talk about our experiences in terms of our hearing loss, and it's been so light and funny and positive. We are going to be meeting each other for coffee soon, and I'm really looking forward to beginning my first friendship with a hearing impaired person.   F 91

Deaf/Signing Friends

The remaining thirty-nine (nearly two-thirds) of the Solitary Mainstream Project participants have left the solitary mainstream behind. They have mastered sign language and now spend a significant portion of their time with other deaf and hard of hearing people or hearing people who know sign language. I cannot claim that my sample of sixty adults is random or that it represents all deaf and hard of hearing individuals educated in the mainstream as solitaires. Qualitative studies, unless there are many of them examining the same phenomenon, do not allow us to make sweeping generalizations about the population of interest. So I cannot claim that for every one hundred solitaires, sixty will choose as adults to learn sign and associate with other d/Deaf individuals. I do hope, however, that the fact that two-thirds of this highly educated and articulate group did choose to learn to sign and include other deaf and hard of hearing people as well as hearing signers in their lives will help to dispel the myth that the Deaf community is only a crutch for those who have no recourse.

These individuals, including the one excerpted below, have done just as I have done. They have sought out and availed themselves of other d/Deaf people, particularly signing Deaf (and hearing) people. Because they have done this for themselves, they now have the option of "leaving" the world of "struggling to understand" for a spell to enjoy leisure and social activities where communication is not an issue. They continue to have hearing neighbors and coworkers, but now they have choices about the nature of their social lives.

> Today is the total opposite of what my social life was like growing up! I'm involved as an officer of a couple of deaf clubs. I play various sports on an all-deaf team. I'm assistant coach for a mostly deaf softball team and was captain for an all-deaf basketball team. I see my deaf friends about three times a week in large gatherings. Of course, knowing sign language now helps too. :) Even my husband is deaf.   F 87

I wish to make very clear the fact that although many referred to spending the bulk of their time with others who use sign language, these "others" clearly include hearing signers as well. In fact, more than several participants mention that all of their current hearing friends know sign. These friends are often interpreters, professionals who are involved with deaf and hard of hearing people, or CODAs (Children of Deaf Adults). These participants are not saying that all their friends are deaf or hard of hearing, but that they all use sign language to communicate with friends, whether those friends are deaf, hard of hearing, or hearing.

My leisure/social involvement with deaf and hard of hearing persons is like living in the deaf world. I work for a private nonprofit organization serving the deaf, hard of hearing, and late-deafened adult. Half of the staff is deaf, hard of hearing, and late-deafened adults. Most of the hearing staff are fluent in sign language. My social life is filled with my deaf friends and their hearing or deaf children. I also have hearing friends, but most of them are CODAS, interpreters, or professionals in deaf-related fields. I have very few hearing friends that don't have anything to do with deaf world. My husband and I don't do social/leisure activities with them as often as we do with our deaf friends.   F 86

The participants of this study who are also parents are very involved with their children's lives. And, those who live in major metropolitan areas or where there are large, active deaf schools or college programs frequently organize family gatherings centered around their children.

We have busy lives with three growing children. So, most of our time is occupied with their needs and activities. We carve out time to go to church, which is a Deaf church, and do monthly activities with this group. I teach sign language to continuing education adults for a local school district one night a week. We help out at the local high school where they have started a "Contact" sign class. We are on a team that travels around the state doing Deaf fairs and track meets. We were involved in a silent dinner group that met every month, but that has been disbanded since the director moved away.   F 86

In the next excerpt, the female participant conveys an interesting twist. When her hearing children were young, they enjoyed the many gatherings that their Deaf parents organized, frequently called KODA activities.[3] These gatherings often involve families that live relatively far from each other, so the children who are assembled are likely not schoolmates. When these children get older, they will naturally want to spend more time with their school or neighborhood friends, who will most likely not be KODAs. This presents a dilemma for the Deaf parents, one that they accept with a modicum of chagrin or sadness.

When our kids were young, most parties were with other KODAs, and we would thereby have a chance to see our deaf friends frequently. Now that our kids are older, their activities are more geared towards their classmates in school. That means more "hearing" parties, and we see our deaf friends less. This forces us to contact hearing parents more now for our kids' activities. It's not too bad because some of them are pretty understanding and do make an effort to communicate with us.   F 80

Many of the solitary mainstream participants describe their lives as very active. I have often marveled at the great depth of social engagement available within the Deaf community. Perhaps this is because so many hearing people seem to think that being deaf couldn't possibly be fun. It is particularly striking to be aware of both this rich social life available within the Deaf community and the pervasive contrasting belief that being deaf is, in and of itself, isolating. The lives of the participants of the Solitary Mainstream Project and the lives of countless others illustrate that this is an erroneous belief.

As the following excerpt demonstrates, there are many activities within which one can become involved. Although major metropolitan areas will offer more to do, motivated parents and d/Deaf adults can find or initiate activities in less-populated areas, if they so desire.

Today, I am an actress with a deaf theatre company. I spend every day mixing with both deaf and hearing adults in my workplace. I feel SO lucky to be here. When we go on tours, I meet young deaf children, and some have never met a deaf adult! A big reflection of what I used to feel. Hearing children love to meet us because we broaden their understanding of our culture and language. They still see us as "different" in some ways, but they become less apprehensive and judgmental when it comes to meeting other deaf people. I also meet parents of deaf children . . . and freely answer any of their questions about my background. I think that they're checking me out and comparing me to their deaf kid. I usually spend my social time with other actors, going to bars, bowling, seeing movies, or hanging out at home. I don't know any other deaf people here in our small and rural town. Usually on breaks, I fly to [cities] to be with my other deaf friends. I also like to fly out to deaf art festivals. I wish I knew more deaf people here. The nearest deaf club is all the way up in [city]! So we do our best to keep each other company here. I usually drive to New York City to catch the latest Broadway shows, and usually there is a mix of hearing and deaf people in our group.   F 83

As mentioned earlier, the participants who indicated that they spend most of their time with other d/Deaf people actually include hearing friends who sign within their mental picture of their social circle. Some appear quite content to have no contact with nonsigning hearing people, with the exception of family members. Just as many, however, acknowledge that they grew up with hearing people and thereby derive some comfort from the hearing world. They further lament, as in the following excerpts, that with nonsigning family members and friends, communication is difficult.

> While I still have a few hearing friends, we don't get together as much as I do with my deaf friends. Main reason: communication. Lately, I've missed the hearing contact because I grew up with it, and I like the balance of getting the best of both worlds. I enjoy doing things with hearing people, and I can't see myself having zero hearing friends. My husband and I would like to have more hearing friends because he, too, grew up in a hearing world the first eleven years of his life and can't just shrug it off.   F 87

> I attend Deaf events as often as I can. I have only two close Deaf friends that I see regularly and many Deaf acquaintances that live far away. My regular everyday life is hearing, and I use voice, not sign. Work environment is completely hearing and very frustrating. I wish it wasn't so much work to remind people of my needs. There are some people I truly enjoy and have great conversations with when in a quiet environment, but when they ask over and over to go out to a bar or out to dinner, it saddens me. My hearing family is far enough away that it isn't frustrating often. But when I see them, it is frustrating. They have forgotten the way to communicate to me. They forget to look at me when talking, to speak loud and clear, etc.   F 91

Most signing Deaf communities of significant size tend to be in major metropolitan areas or near deaf schools or colleges. This fact is a barrier to involvement for some. Naturally, people can only live where they can find employment, and other factors may come into play as well. The excerpt below echoes more than a few of the participants who stated their desire to live near more d/Deaf people.

Since [my wife and I] live in a small city, we don't see as many deaf folks as we'd like. Nor do we have the social opportunities we'd have in a larger Deaf community. At this time, we don't have much choice. But within the next few years, we hope to relocate to a city/metro area with a much larger Deaf community. That's probably the main change I'd like to see in my social life.   M 87

Finally, a few participants, like the one excerpted below, commented on their general desire to develop closer friendships with people. They surmised that the social isolation of the solitary mainstream during their K–12 years has negatively influenced their adulthood, making it difficult for them to form close relationships.

Now, my leisure/social life is primarily with signing Deaf or (signing hearing) people. I go to sign-interpreted plays, Deaf plays and events, and the like. But, I have noticed that I have a hard time entering a new Deaf community and making friends. Part of it could be the cliquishness of some Deaf people, but I think a large part of it is a remnant of my experiences in the mainstream. Because I was so socially isolated, I only made one or two "friends" in the mainstream. And I have noticed that even in the Deaf community, I usually have only one or two real friends that I hold onto at a time. Also, the trauma of the abuse during middle school has made me somewhat reserved, and I am slow to open up to people enough to establish a real friendship. I can be friendly and have a superficial conversation with many people that I know at Deaf events, but the relationship usually doesn't go further than that on a more intimate, interpersonal level. I do wish I could develop more friendships, but currently, I really don't have any real friendships in the community where I live. (I do have friendships with others, but on a long-distance basis, which is insufficient.) My one real friendship now is with my wife (who is hearing, but signs), and we stay home together a lot.   M 81

The Perfect Balance

So there are, in fact, two worlds: Deaf and hearing. As an adult who spent the first twenty years of her life as a solitaire and the next thirty immersed in both worlds alternately, I can see the advantages of both. I believe that all deaf and hard of hearing children deserve to learn about the Deaf world as well as the hearing world. They deserve a viable choice, one that holds up each world as equally important and equally valuable. Given such a choice, I believe that most, if not all, deaf and hard of hearing people will choose to be involved with both.

I am very satisfied with my social/leisure time now. I have several deaf and several hearing friends. There is quite a good balance between the number of deaf friends and hearing friends I have. I often see my deaf friends at church-related functions and deaf club events. My hearing friends are seen at work and at evening get-togethers (suppers, etc.). Most of my hearing friends know sign language, which is the language we use to communicate. I do have a girl-friend who is hearing, and we spend a majority of our time together. I do spend some time alone, too. I love to read, write, and listen to music. I also enjoy going to the local YMCA. I could not imagine my leisure time being any different. I have a good mix of people and activities. M 93

I pretty much spend my leisure time with both communities (hard of hearing and normal). Why? First of all, my reason for hanging out with hearing folks is to maintain my social standing among them. I need them in order to have a wider variety of new opportunities that might interest me. Of course, I'll continue to struggle with communication, but this also provides the hearing people with an opportunity interact with me. In other words, it's an education for everyone. I usually go to parties with other deaf and hard of hearing folks, which provides me with a recharge in self-esteem (I can go out and do things my way). At this time, the majority of my friends are hard of hearing because we provide emotional support and encourage each other to survive out there. I do have some close friends who are not hard of hearing, but they have a lot of motiva-tion to learn how to socialize with me. I don't mind educating them if they are willing to learn. There are times when there are no parties where I can recharge. I spend some quality time alone. When I do spend some time alone, I tend to focus on new opportunities or think about those events where I need to take control of the situation. In other words, I try to think of new ways to promote myself as an individual who just wants to be me and not someone [who is] handicapped. Personally, I think I do rather well in balancing my involvement with both sides. It's been a

learning experience that will never stop. I'll continue to grow with each
situation that I get myself into.   F 83

Not every d/Deaf person is able to live near a major metropolitan area
that is teeming with activities planned by and for deaf and hard of hearing
individuals. Not every d/Deaf person has the personal characteristics or circumstances to live a life like some of the more active participants of the Solitary Mainstream Project. Still, most of these individuals seem to have three
wishes: They would like their hearing family and friends to learn to sign;
they would like to live closer to more signers (deaf, hard of hearing, or hearing); and they would like to have an easier time finding and making close
friends. Most of them have managed to carve out a life containing at least
some of these elements. Through their own persistent efforts, they have
found an oasis from which to drink, from which to recharge.

In the next few chapters, I will talk more about my own adult life and
particularly, how I enjoy the best of both worlds. Although so much of my
life is full of involvement outside of my home, I do have an anchor in my
husband, Rick Baldi, whom I married in 1992. Rick was also educated as
a solitaire, although to me, his story is even more painful than my own.
From his story and that of a few other male former solitaires I came to
know through Rick and also through my students at Gallaudet, I believe
that deaf and hard of hearing boys face even more challenges in the public school arena.

Rick's mother, to her great credit, was determined to get the best possible education for her son, who was born in early 1952 with a severe hearing loss (about 75–80 dB in both ears). She pretty much single-handedly
was responsible for the establishment of a small oral program near their
hometown, Haddonfield, New Jersey. In this program were children of
various ages, and Rick tells me they spent hours of each day with headphones on, practicing speech. After school, the parents of these children
were responsible for, essentially, teaching them the rest of the important
school subjects (e.g., reading, writing, and arithmetic).

There were usually about nine children in this program. Rick is still in
touch with several of them, despite the fact that when he was nine, he was
deemed ready for the mainstream and literally dumped (to hear him tell

Marrying Rick was a package deal that included his children Justin and Jessica.

it) into the local elementary school. From that point on, his education was a sham. He didn't understand what was going on around him, and as a boy, he quickly learned that it was not cool to ask for repetition or help. So he essentially was passed through and had determined by the time he was a teenager that he was destined to pump gas at the local filling station.

Fortuitously, a high school guidance counselor, who was himself hard of hearing, suggested that Rick apply to Gallaudet University. Ironically, we both arrived at Gallaudet in the fall of 1971, but we ran in different circles and were never more than acquaintances. Years later, in 1985 actually, we were introduced by a mutual friend who knew we had a lot in common. Truthfully, we do have an awful lot in common, more even than this book reveals. Such has kept us together through thick and thin, as the saying goes, and the future looks bright. Today, Rick is in the "Never Too Late Club" at Gallaudet, almost done with his master's degree in social work as of this writing. Consider him a late bloomer.

One of the nice things about being married to Rick is that he was a "package deal," as he so aptly put it. At the time we met, his daughter Jessica was just a year old, and his son Justin was three.

When I turned forty, my biological clock was clanging like there was no tomorrow. To make a long story short, I decided that my life was so very entwined with Rick and his children that there was no sense in fixing what was not broken. One could say I am childless mostly by choice. My life is so full I don't have time to regret it, and I would gamble that day will never come for me. There is far too much to do, let alone the fact that I did gain an instant family.

Because of our shared background, Rick and I have always felt that we understand each other's struggles and strengths like perhaps few others could. Before meeting each other, we each had twenty years to evolve as former solitaires, and then chose to become immersed in the Deaf community. And we continue to evolve as individuals as well as evolving as a couple.

There is enough for a whole other book revolved around our relationship. Suffice it to say that we understand and appreciate each other's need for alone time, one-on-one time, and time with small groups of mutual friends. Neither of us outgrew that comfort with solitude, with just one friend or just a few friends. We travel, hike, ski and snowboard, dance, swim and talk, talk, and talk some more. Our close circle is made up of signers—mostly deaf or hard of hearing—but a few cherished hearing friends are in the mix as well.

7

The Best of Both Worlds

My visits and then immersion in the oasis of the Deaf world began that fortuitous day at Washington College when I spotted the animated chatter of the Deaf soccer players across the cafeteria. Since I chose at age twenty to open myself to the Deaf world, I have truly been able to mold my life around the opportunities provided by both the Deaf and hearing worlds. I am very grateful for having had all of these options, and for all the people who shared these experiences with me, in *both worlds*.

I fear I give the impression that I care only for the Deaf world. That is not so. In chapter 8, I share some of my rich experiences I have had in the hearing world since becoming aware of the Deaf world. I fully recognize that through my one-on-one relationships with my parents, siblings, a few teachers, and a few close friends, I have a level of comfort with the hearing world. There are parts of the Deaf world that are alien to me, as there are parts of the hearing world that are alien to me. And, there are aspects of the Deaf world that I dearly love, and there are also aspects of the hearing world that I dearly love.

This chapter is focused on my relationships with two young women, Jessica and Summer, who are both a part of my inner circle today, and who I think so well represent the best of both worlds.

Jessica: Sort-of Like Me

Justin was eight and Jessica was six when I married their father Rick in 1992. They are now adults, and I count them as dear to me. Justin and Jessica taught me much about two elements of the Deaf community. Justin, being hearing, is a CODA (Child of Deaf Adults) and Jessica, by virtue of her mother's line, is a DOD (Deaf of Deaf).

In chapter 2, I discussed how CODAs are privy to how hearing people view d/Deaf people. And although Justin is hearing, I think of him as part of my Deaf world. He thinks likewise. My relationship with Jessica has taught me about the core of the Deaf community, the DODs.

I first met Jessica when she was not yet three years old. Her proud papa brought her over to meet me one lovely summer day. She had on the cutest little blue flowery outfit. This was probably the first time I had a deaf child in my house. Little Jessica was very personable, as she remains today. With her dark curly hair and lovely little face, she was captivating from the start. Rick and I decided to take her to a playground, and she followed me upstairs to my bedroom so I could change into more appropriate shoes. I had a pair of sneakers for each activity: racquetball, running, aerobics, walking, and gardening, and my shoes were all neatly lined up on my closet floor. When Jessica looked at them, her eyes grew wider by the second. She looked up at me and signed in fluent ASL with her pudgy little hands, complete with appropriate facial expression, WHOSE SHOES ARE THOSE? I looked at her and signed MINE with a facial expression that said, "But of course!" Her eyes grew about as wide as humanly possible as she signed back ALL OF THEM? with a facial expression that said, "That's impossible!"

Her facial expression included a specific mouth movement that is well known to native ASL users. This mouth movement conveys the idea "They can't possibly ALLLL be yours!" The incredulous look on her face matched the mouth movement so precisely, as one might expect from a much more mature language user. I will never forget how stunned I was that she was able to appropriately use a slang sign that had a very intricate meaning and that her language was so evolved at her young age that she could convey this nuance. It would be like a hearing two-year-old saying,

"Oh Mom, get real!" at a culturally appropriate moment. I realized then that my knowledge of ASL was going to increase exponentially if I continued to spend time with this preschooler.

Another remarkable incident occurred around Christmas just a few years later when Jessica was four. I already knew that she loved music and loved to sign songs.[1] We were sitting at our dining room table, singing and signing—me, Rick, Jessica, Justin, and a few other adult friends. I was plunking out the tunes on a small synthesizer, and Rick and Jessica were signing "Silent Night." I hit a wrong key. I stopped playing and signed,

The first day I met Jessica, I was astounded at her nuanced signing ability.

OOPS, SORRY, I GOOFED. Jessica immediately got this "Oh, I understand" expression on her face, and she triumphantly and emphatically finger-spelled, REWIND! Not only did she fingerspell it clearly and distinctly, but she used another ASL feature, this time in the way she moved her hand up and down as she spelled it, to convey that she was "making an announce-ment." Once again, she used a fine nuance of the language in a unique and frankly hilarious way.

We shared lots of music-related things. Of her "four parents," I was probably the one most attuned to music, and it was fun to share that with her. Jessica loved to dance, sing, and sign songs. We would often be in the car doing errands and she would want to sing (really *sing*, with our voices) while we drove. Imagine the mixed feelings in my heart when one sum-mer day, as we were driving with the windows down, she said, LET'S SING! I said, O, FIRST, ROLL UP THE WINDOWS, and she asked WHY?

That was one of the hardest questions I have ever had to answer.

When all is said and done, Jessica made a believer out of me. The truth about ASL is that until you really know it, you cannot appreciate it. Unfortunately, its stigma as an inferior language coerces us not to think of it as a real language until we learn enough of it to see that it is equal to yet different from spoken language.

As I got to know Jessica, my knowledge of and respect for ASL went from almost nonexistent to profound. My interactions with her also prompted me to learn more about the people known in the community as DODs. Jes-sica's mother is Deaf; in fact Jessica is the fourth known generation of deaf girls in her mother's line. In her family's genetic pattern of deafness, the girls are deaf and the boys are hearing. Early on, I could see that Jessica's experi-ence as a Deaf child was different from mine. Not only did she have two Deaf parents (and two Deaf stepparents for that matter), but she attended a Deaf school. So, all her friends were Deaf. And the great majority of her par-ents' friends were either Deaf or hearing signers. Definitely not a solitaire.

In Jessica, I saw firsthand the beneficial effects of a Deaf child growing up in a bilingual environment. It was bilingual because although most of the adults around her have been Deaf, all four parents (and many friends as well) are actually bilingual—they use both ASL and English. She first attended Kendall School (on the Gallaudet campus) in a class full of other bilingual DODs, and then later the Maryland School for the Deaf. She is equally proficient in ASL and English. She is comfortable with herself. She has been involved in many extracurricular activities, always with other children who can sign and with whom she can identify.

For a while, I thought I could really identify with Jessica. But then I met another young girl who made me realize that while I could identify with Jessica for her deafness per se, I did not identify with her in another very important way.

Summer: Really Like Me

One November day in 1989, I found myself sitting in a hotel banquet hall in Indianapolis. The gentleman at my right, Richard Keelor, explained that he was my host for this luncheon, given in honor of the ten of us who were being inducted into the National Fitness Leaders Association. My interpreter sat to his right, but he was easy to lipread, so I didn't need to rely on her. He told me, "I think our meeting is divinely intentioned; I have a friend who has a deaf daughter. The girl just had a cochlear implant, and I want you to meet them both."

I politely nodded my head and said, "Oh, wonderful. I would love to meet them." I asked some polite questions such as "Where do they live?" and "How old is the girl?" But in the back of my head I was thinking "Oh no! Not another one of these parents who wants their child to become hearing." Often in the past, people have asked me to meet their deaf relative or acquaintance, saying, "My friend (or child) is deaf too, but she doesn't speak as well as you do. Maybe you could help her?" When I met parents of deaf children, their minds were frequently really closed to the Deaf community. I was to be pleasantly surprised to find that this wasn't the case with Mr. Keelor's friend Linda Crider. Linda's relationship with her deaf daughter Summer can serve as a model for all hearing families with deaf children. And the entire relationship, still unfolding to this day, has enriched my own life in ways I could not have imagined.

I first met Summer when she was seven or eight years old. From that time, her mother would invite me to visit each of the schools she attended.

First there was a special classroom for deaf and hard of hearing children in a local elementary school. Then there were a few years in a private school. Then there was a "lab school" affiliated with the state university, where she spent most of her solitary years. At each of these schools, I observed her in her classroom for several hours. It is hard to describe what I saw because I did not like what I saw. I felt sorry for Summer. Frankly, I couldn't even see her capabilities during those years and worried for her future. She was always so quiet and in the background. The fact that she was so tall for her age didn't help her appearance. I felt angry at the situation and for knowing there were few options for a mother who, like all mothers, was loathe to send her child to a boarding school.

Richard Keelor made a match that led to many special memories and continues to do so. Less than two years after our meeting, Linda and I produced *Shape Up 'n Sign*, a videotape that enables children (and adults) to learn a little sign language while getting a moderate workout as well. Jessica, Justin, and Summer appear in this video along with a few of Summer's schoolmates. Linda was in the fitness field, as I was at the time. This project gave us and our families several opportunities to get together when the children were young.

I must credit Linda for her steadfast efforts to remain in touch with me and my family. She had really wanted Summer to have as much experience as possible with both Deaf and hearing people, so that as an adult, Summer would know what choices were open to her. As such, she paved the way for Summer's eventual ability to mold her environment to fit her needs.

Over the span of Summer's K–12 years, Linda often agonized about where to place her deaf daughter; thus, Summer attended four different schools over this time period. Linda's words best describe Summer's education up until her sophomore year of high school.

> Basically, they (the first public school Summer entered) were NOT supportive of the implant. Their "hearing impaired" program involved an excellent "self-contained" program, and when I asked to have her "mainstreamed" for several academic classes, they were less than prepared. I would find her sitting in the back of the mainstream classroom with her

Making the *Shape Up 'n Sign* video.

back to the teacher, facing an interpreter, at a separate table from the rest of the hearing kids. Obviously they "didn't get it." I tried getting them set up with consultants to understand better the mainstreaming concept, but they resisted. I think things have changed since then. . . . hopefully. That was around 1991–1992. At [the small private school], she was happy but lost ground because of their philosophy—no textbooks and everything is done orally. At this time, I personally hired [Summer's first interpreter] (the school could ill afford to pay for interpreter. . . . They were a small struggling private school). Two years later, she was accepted into [Summer's second public school]. She had no interpreters in the fourth to seventh grade, but excellent teachers who reorganized their teaching techniques to include her needs . . . overheads for much of the teacher's information . . . handouts, reading, individual one-on-one. [This worked very well—Summer grew a lot during those years—even though looking back now, Summer will tell you she still missed the class discussions]. . . . But I knew once she started high school with lectures and many different teachers, she would be

lost. So that is when I insisted on a sign language OR oral interpreter. . . .
No one knowing anything about the second category. I settled for a sign
language interpreter and then spent months tracking them down, for three
consecutive years. . . . Some good some not so good, and the school reluctant, but willing to pay. One of these interpreters was really special and
Summer really loved her. Summer commented that she was very good as a
social interpreter—that was important for her. She was the one who taught
Summer ASL and helped her to accept her deafness in a hearing world.[2]

My reasons for including this degree of detail about Linda and Summer
are threefold. First, I want to illustrate what one mother did to ensure that
her daughter's needs were met. Linda is a well-educated, self-starting,
ambitious woman. Many mothers would be hard pressed to have the personal and social resources to be so involved in their children's lives. Linda
was a single mother with two other children who had to work exhaustively
with the educational system in her town to ensure Summer received a
good education. A parent should not have to do this. And many parents
do not have the resources or the energy to do what Linda did.

Second, Summer's story also demonstrates that even by the 1990s, little
had changed for solitaires. She entered school in 1988, after the Education
for all Handicapped Children Act had been in effect for almost fifteen
years. Until she left her local school system in 1998, that system was still
unable to provide all that she needed in spite of Linda's steadfast advocacy
efforts.

Summer decided that her public school was not meeting her needs and
took matters into her own hands at a younger age than I did. Thanks to
her mother's persistent search for opportunities for her daughter, Summer
learned of Gallaudet University's Young Scholars Program. I was elated
when she decided to attend, knowing that I would see both her and her
mother before and after this month-long session. For as long as we had
been in touch, I saw it as my job to educate both of them about the benefits of affiliation with the Deaf community. Now, Summer would have an
immersion experience of her own.

After spending a month with other capable and ambitious Deaf peers,
Summer returned home a changed person. During her first week of tenth

Summer's graduation was an exciting and emotional experience for me.

grade back in her local school, she approached her mother and declared, "I want to transfer to the Florida School for the Deaf and Blind [FSDB]."

In May 2002, Linda invited me down to St. Augustine to attend Summer's graduation from FSDB, where she gave the valedictory address. Little did I realize it would represent a major epiphany in my own life.

Summer, a willowy Nordic type, looked lovely in her white cap and gown. Her height had become an asset rather than a liability. The Florida school had an entire weekend of festivities, including entertainment by the graduating seniors. On Thursday evening, the seniors put on a dance performance. Summer and her graduating friends were signing songs and dancing and celebrating. Saturday morning there was a brunch, and then graduation, and then dinner. At the actual commencement, Summer gave the valediction.

I cried through most of her address, especially toward the end when she held up the I-LOVE-YOU sign, a sign that has become universally known and gave her analysis of what it really meant.

We will all, sooner or later, realize what our "famous Deaf sign" really means. [This sign, the I-LOVE-YOU sign] is the greatest "Hello" and the greatest "See you later." I refuse to say "Goodbye," because I believe we are going to bump into each other. This sign doesn't mean "I love you. Goodbye;" this sign is the greatest "See you later," because I know I will see all of you again in the future somewhere. [3]

Then I understood why I wept. I was so happy for her, that she had had a rich and fruitful high school experience. She had friends, extracurricular activities, fun—the whole experience. Her high school years were as everyone's high school years should be. There she was in her two worlds: the world of her loving hearing family, and the world of her loving Deaf friends. I cried tears of joy for the wonderful and rich high school experience she had, and that I helped to make it so. And I cried tears of regret that I had not had anything even close to this high school experience.

It was then that I realized how very much I identified with her. She was like me, and I was like her. And because she joined the Deaf world at age fifteen instead of twenty-one, she had a rich high school experience and is now having a rich college experience at Gallaudet. She will always be able to choose the best of both the hearing and the Deaf worlds.

For even having a Deaf world to include in our choices, Summer and I both owe a debt of gratitude to Jessica's people.

Jessica's People: Deaf of Deaf

In chapter 1, I explained that regardless of their desire to do what was best for me, neither my parents nor anyone at Cos Cob School knew what I needed in the way of support. And I would hazard an educated guess that this scenario is playing itself out all over the United States and the world. It may be that in America there is a greater awareness of hearing loss and certainly a political consciousness that children with disabilities of any kind ought to have the same opportunities as their able bodied peers. In America and other more developed countries, deaf and hard of hearing children may be having more positive academic experiences. Still, when it comes down to concrete actions to reduce social isolation, the parents, the teachers, and certainly the deaf children born to hearing families don't know what to do. When a deaf child is born into a hearing family, it is usually a new and distressing experience for that family. When a deaf child enters a public school, it may very well be a new and distressing experience for his teachers as well.

But the birth of a deaf child is not novel—in fact it is a cause for rejoicing for one group of people: those known as "Deaf of Deaf" (DOD). These are Jessica's people, and it took me a very long time to come to know them, and to feel comfortable with them. It is because of stigma that it took me so long, for which I am sorry. Today I have the utmost respect for and gratitude toward this stalwart group of survivors.

The story of my relationship with DODs probably goes back to my first few days on the Gallaudet campus, when I realized that there seemed to be two different ways of signing. One way involved actually speaking and then signing along with the speaking. Often the speaking was soundless, like lip-synching. Signers of this bent would actually mouth out the English words and sign simultaneously. So, the signs become an adjunct to lipreading, and this works well for individuals who are fluent in English.

When people used this kind of signing, I understood them. I would read their lips, and I quickly learned sign vocabulary as it was associated with English words and sentences. The Gallaudet students who used this form of sign language, I quickly learned, were like me in that they had come from the hearing world. They had been solitaires, or they had been in some mainstream programs. Or, they might have been people who very recently lost their hearing. And, many of Gallaudet's hearing teachers and staff members used this kind of signing.

The other way of signing was fast and accentuated by animated facial expressions. I found it fascinating to watch even if it was indecipherable to me. Eventually, I learned that this was American Sign Language. I also learned that, back in the early 1970s, most of the students who used this kind of sign language came from residential schools. Indeed, many years later, young Jessica would use ASL to ask me about "ALLLLLL" those shoes.

During my twenties, I spent all my free time catching up on the social life that I missed during my K–12 years. I did not seek out any of those "residential school folks" (as I thought of them) simply because I had plenty of friends who had been solitaires like me. Having grown up in the midst of undecipherable conversation, why would I subject myself to more of such? No, I chose to interact with those who were most like me and with whom I could easily converse regardless of how many people were involved and how much background noise was present. I didn't go looking for residential school folks with whom to become friends, and they didn't come looking for me.

It was not that I did not respect the residential school folks before seeing Jessica's flair for language. I just hadn't taken the time to get to know any of them. I think that in addition to simply following my comfort zone, I was influenced by all those terrible attitudes toward d/Deaf people described in previous chapters. I got the impression from the rest of the world, in some subtle ways, that ASL was an inferior language and that those residential school folks were probably not as smart as the rest of us.

Because of Jessica and a few other individuals, my mind was opened. I learned that my bias against ASL was wrong. DODs are very smart and resourceful. And they have taken care of their own. Although they make up only 10 percent of the total deaf and hard of hearing population, they have led the way since the beginning of the Deaf community. While it was a very long time before I became well-versed enough in ASL that I could follow a conversation between fluent users, I nevertheless came to realize that I owe the DODs and their forebears a great debt for the richness of my life today.

The Advantaged Few

When I was in the planning stages for the Solitary Mainstream Project, I quickly saw a dilemma of sorts with how to treat solitaires from Deaf families. I felt that their life experience, even how they would exist inside the solitary mainstream, would be different from that of Deaf of Hearing people (DOHs), like me. After all, DODs presumably had parents who understood what they were going through. Their parents could, more than any hearing parent, provide much more empathy and perhaps offer concrete suggestions about problems and situations the children encountered. And, I knew that these DOD solitaires grew up with an extended family of Deaf relatives, including CODAs, so surely they would have been among peers who could sign. Within this peer group, I surmised that they would have rarely found themselves in the situation of being unable to understand the conversations going on around them. I felt there were too many essential differences between DODs and DOHs to include both in my study without distinguishing them. I decided that I could not do justice to their story and thus focused only on Deaf of Hearing solitaires.

I did, however, have the good fortune to become acquainted with Tom Holcomb, a Deaf of Deaf scholar who approached me after seeing a presentation I did at a conference. He was interested in the public school experience, having noticed and expounded on the fact that many of the Deaf students in his Deaf Studies classes at Ohlone College were former solitaires, although he did not yet have a label for them. I asked Dr. Holcomb if he might help me understand how DOD children experienced the solitary mainstream. In essence, he told me his story—some of which I will share here. It illustrates how truly different life is for DODs compared with that of most d/Deaf individuals, 90 percent of whom are born to hearing parents. In the following quote, he describes the lives of four generations of Deaf people living what he calls "a life of full inclusion."

> All my life, I was surrounded by deaf people. They were wonderful role models for me, and I learned early on that it's indeed dandy to be deaf. I have an older brother who is deaf. My maternal grandparents were deaf as well, and I was fortunate enough to be very close to them. Both my grandparents had a combination of deaf and hearing siblings. The majority of the hearing relatives could sign, so practically everyone in the family experienced a life of full inclusion regardless of their hearing status. Never for a minute did I wonder if my life would be better if I were hearing. I was totally content with my deaf experience and, in fact, I often felt fortunate and grateful that I was a member of this special, warm and caring community known as the Deaf community.
>
> My family roots can be traced to Akron, Ohio, the rubber capital of the world. Because of the numerous factories located in the city, it became a magnet for deaf people during the world wars as jobs were plentiful since the majority of hearing men had gone to serve the country. My grandparents separately migrated to Akron in the early 1900s after graduating from the

North Carolina School for the Deaf and the Pennsylvania School for the Deaf and met and married there. They devoted forty years of their lives to serving their country by working on the assembly lines at the Goodyear factory. Here they became part of the active, vibrant Deaf community.

My grandparents gave birth to two girls, one deaf (my mother) and one hearing (my aunt). Both girls brought much joy regardless of their hearing status. My grandparents were able to provide them with the communication tools of both a signed language and English, and because of this, both my mother and her sister were fluent in ASL and English. In spite of my mother's inability to hear, communication within the home and in society at large was really never an issue for her. Furthermore, she was fortunate enough to be surrounded by many outstanding deaf people in the community. They were well respected in their professions and for their leadership in community affairs. Because of the high number of deaf leaders, the state was able to provide an outstanding education for young deaf children at the Ohio School for the Deaf. The school was one of a few deaf schools that were accredited during those days.[4]

What a different story! Tom thus thinks of himself as one of a long line of Deaf individuals who have crafted what he calls "tools for effective living" for Deaf individuals living in a predominantly hearing world. Listening to his take on inclusion coupled with his stories demonstrating the self-advocating efforts of his parents and grandparents, I came to fully appreciate just how squarely the vibrancy that pervades the Deaf community sits on the shoulders of people like the Holcombs of earlier generations. I came to appreciate that it is the Deaf of Deaf who had fashioned an excellent and truly inclusive model for deaf and hard of hearing children long ago. Tom's parents fashioned such a model for him, ten years before Public Law 94–142 was passed. For a glimpse of the example they set, I am including a bit more of Tom's description of his solitary mainstream years.

I was eight years old when my family moved to California. At that time, the school for the deaf in Riverside had a long waiting list, so my brother and I had to attend a local mainstream program with approximately fifty deaf students in self-contained classes. Because of my academic skills, it was determined that I needed to be mainstreamed on a full-time basis. My parents came up with an idea, one that was unheard of and perhaps considered bizarre during those days.

Instead of expecting me to adapt to the "hearing" environment, they suggested several things to make the classroom inclusive for everyone. Their idea for an inclusive environment included teaching the hearing students and teachers how to sign in addition to employing a sign language interpreter to help facilitate communication between the deaf student (me) and the class. To the school's credit, they bought into the idea, and a crash course in signing and deaf awareness was implemented. A sign language interpreter was hired. I believe it was the very first time anywhere in the world that a sign language interpreter was employed to facilitate communication in a classroom at the elementary level.

My elementary school experience was so positive that I chose to continue my education at a local junior high school as a solitaire. Unfortunately, the two years at the junior high school were the most lonely and isolating time in my life. I was cut off from the support of my deaf peers (who were in the self-contained program) who had been readily available to me at the elementary school. I did not realize at that time how invaluable their support was in terms of keeping me grounded and happy. In addition, instead of being in a class with my friends and teachers who took time to learn sign language, I had to deal with rotating classes, each with different students and teachers whose attitudes varied towards me as a deaf person.

By the time I was done with my junior high career, my self-esteem was battered, my self-confidence plummeted, my identity became confused, and my outlook towards life became bleak. I desperately wanted a change, and fortunately, my parents moved again, this time to the East Coast. I had the opportunity to attend an exemplary program called the Model Secondary School for the Deaf in Washington, D.C. This federally sponsored program was created for people just like me—solitaires and other deaf students who were in need of more appropriate educational stimulation. There, my experiences as a solitaire ended, and a happy, well-adjusted, and secure existence was mine once again.[5]

Although I had heard along the wayside that Deaf of Deaf individuals traditionally passed Deaf culture to Deaf of Hearing in residential schools, my full recognition of the profound and personal implications of this phenomenon is fairly recent. It did not hit home until after I had years of involvement with Jessica, many books under my belt, and numerous conversations with Tom Holcomb and a few other Deaf of Deaf individuals who were educated as solitaires. In these conversations, I learned about how they are presently advocating for their own Deaf children. In chapter 9, I share examples of how some other Deaf of Deaf individuals are promoting their own Deaf children's involvement in the hearing mainstream. These examples can inspire the rest of us.

Let the Children Know

Summer's valedictory address struck an important note—particularly her comments about the I-LOVE-YOU sign being the "greatest see you later"— which echoed the sentiments expressed by Henry Rider 150 years earlier when he made reference to Deaf community gatherings as "oases to the famished traveler." Perhaps that is the essence of the Deaf community—knowing one never needs to say good-bye, because there will always be another chance to meet at a deaf school reunion, at Deaf festivals (held all over the United States), at the World Games for the Deaf (held in various host countries, just like the Olympics), or at Deaf Way III.[6] Deaf and hard of hearing children need to know about these resources, which have great potential for enriching their sense of place and enhancing life satisfaction.

Because I opened myself to the Deaf world, I feel I have had a vastly different life experience than did my father. Certainly, I have probably a hundred-fold more friends than he had. Instead of cultivating friends, he focused on family and household during his working years, and during his retirement, he made art. He painted hundreds of watercolors and oils, and he made lots of prints on his antique press salvaged from a nearby private school. He also made tables, cabinets, and dollhouses. I know he loved these hobbies. When I would go home for visits, he always beckoned, "Come see what I painted." I always respected his spending time with his art. It seemed to me that his life was solitary and lonely, and art was his one solace. He signed only a handful of his hundreds of works, most of which now live in the nooks and crannies of my house. I hope to honor him some day by finding a way to do something with it all.

Of those hundreds of paintings my father completed during his retirement, the one that serves as the frontispiece for this book has always been one of my favorites. I didn't really know what attracted me to it, as it was unframed and on a plain white background. Now I realize there is a single rose standing out from the rest. Ah! A solitaire!

I do not profess to tell all deaf and hard of hearing adults that they *should* take advantage of both the Deaf and hearing worlds. But I do believe that all deaf and hard of hearing children deserve to be exposed to both. And for deaf and hard of hearing children to be exposed to both, the hearing parents, teachers, and neighbors must be open to learning about deaf and hard of hearing adults and their history. Further, deaf and hard of hearing adults need to make themselves available as mentors, leaders, coaches, advisors, and role models.

The two worlds ought to be presented as equal, though different. Each world offers its own opportunities. All deaf and hard of hearing children should have opportunities in both worlds. Only in that way will they be able to freely choose the depth and breadth of association they wish to achieve in each—for today, for tomorrow, and for the next day.

8

Alone in the Mainstream Again:

Constructing Inclusion

AFTER I had been immersed within the Deaf community for about ten years, I got the itch to venture back out into the mainstream. I have since engaged myself in several such ventures, and it appears all were attempts to participate in some activity that was not available in the Deaf world. Each venture started with an intention to "check it out," so that if I liked the activity and the situation, I could invite some Deaf friends to join me. Ultimately, I wanted to enjoy the new experience in the company of people with whom I could communicate easily.

Over the years, I have come to realize that what I have been doing through these efforts needs to be done all over the United States and, in fact, the world. I have been deliberately constructing effective inclusion for me and my friends.

Situations and environments where deaf and hard of hearing children are truly included will not happen unless adults (both d/Deaf and hearing) design them and then serve as models within them. These children will not be privy to conversations in the locker rooms, the cafeteria, the hallways, or the recreation center unless deaf and hard of hearing adults begin to construct these environments and invite concerned hearing adults (parents, teachers, etc.) to collaborate. Solitary and almost-solitary children will continue to be socially isolated until adults mend the larger milieu.

The stories in this chapter relay my own attempts to make this kind of impact. They demonstrate what truly inclusive situations and environments would look like. I know that other deaf and hard of hearing adults have made similar efforts. We need to continue, expand, and make our efforts known.

I realized in analyzing these experiences that my years in the hearing world gave me just enough comfort, awareness, and survival skills that I would be willing and able to venture out again into that desert—the mainstream. This realization made me a bit more grateful for what I *did* learn during those years.

Essential Skills and Confidence

I must give credit to my mother for instilling a love of learning in me. She was an avid reader, and as soon as I could read "jump Spot jump" we started walking up the street to the library at least once a week. On summer days, we would sit outside on our respective lounge chairs and read the summer away. My mother has probably read a majority of the significant books of the past seventy years, both fiction and nonfiction. I am certain that my love for reading enabled me to pick up as much information as a child possibly could through the printed word.

Dad deserves credit for nurturing my love for athletics, music, nature, and art. He taught me to swim, ride my bike, and play racquet sports at an early age. He taught me to make wooden boats, pull weeds and play the drums. After he died I became interested in art. When he was alive, he and my mother would visit me in Maryland and he would ask "Have you been to any museums lately?" I would say, "Oh Dad, you know I only go there when you are here!" But after he died, I started to appreciate the museums of Washington.

The quiet and orderly school environment of my elementary school and the teachers at Cos Cob School all served me well. At the time, there was an apparent practice of keeping the same teacher for both first and second grade. Mrs. White had one-to-one reading time with me on a regular basis. My third-grade teacher, Mrs. Pickering, noticed that three of us—Joe, Eddie, and me—were far ahead of the rest of the class in arithmetic. So, she put us to work in one corner of the classroom on our own. In a nutshell, I must admit that yes, I had a good academic experience at Cos Cob School. I think this is because I had a moderate hearing loss, most of the information came directly from the teacher, and there were few if any distractions.

In junior high, high school, and college, my hearing loss progressed. I have a general recollection that in junior high I had a 65-dB loss, and by

My mother, Katherine Papaharris Oliva (1919–), upon her high school graduation from Straubenmuller Textile High School at the age of seventeen.

the time I was tested at Gallaudet during my senior year of college, it had progressed to a 95-dB loss. I think this greater hearing loss coupled with the fact that, by seventh grade, I had six to eight teachers to contend with each year, made the academic experience deteriorate as well. In addition, class discussion as a means of learning increased exponentially as I moved

My father, Robert Michael Oliva (1919–1996), upon his retirement at age sixty from the *New York Daily News* in 1979.

into the higher grades. No longer did I get straight As. I got more Bs, and just a few Cs. The Cs would always frustrate me greatly, because I knew that my lack of hearing contributed greatly to them. Most memorable was the fact that in the first half of the first semester of freshman biology at Washington College, I actually received an F. It was a large lecture class, and all the students took notes throughout the class. I did copy another student's notes, but it just wasn't enough to read someone else's notes. I didn't understand one word the teacher said. Through twenty-five hours of studying, I managed to pull that F up to a C by the end of the semester. That put an end to my science career.

Nevertheless, with ample attention to studying and actually reading my textbooks, I managed to graduate from both high school and college with better than a 3.5 average. Thus I developed confidence in my intellect and in my ability to both read and write. That same confidence in myself, my varied interests, and, I suppose, my adventurous nature have spurred me back out into the mainstream to engage in activities that were not yet available in the Deaf world of metropolitan Washington, D.C.

A Past Foray, Full of Sound and Fury, Signifying . . .

My first foray back into the solitary mainstream involved the world of exercise, as initially described in chapter 6. I wanted to play racquetball, so I joined a league and played against hearing women for a few years. I also joined forces with some other Deaf adults and organized Deaf tournaments. Thus, I played a small role in getting Deaf people involved in this sport. Later, I took an aerobics dance class at a local gym, and soon was certified as an aerobics instructor.

This foray into the fitness arena lasted more than fifteen years. It began with my participation as an aerobics dance student for several eight-week sessions at a local community center. I could see that I caught on to the routines faster than most of the other (hearing) students. I thought, "I could be an instructor! Maybe I could set up some classes at Gallaudet!"

I asked how one would go about becoming an instructor and proceeded to go through those channels. On a Friday evening, I showed up with about ten other aspiring instructors—all hearing women, all strangers to me. The owner of the company proceeded to explain the audition procedures. It was quiet and orderly, and she was fairly easy to hear/lipread. She would teach us a routine that evening. On Saturday, we would learn more routines, and on Sunday, we would audition individually. The process sounded easy.

So there I was, following along as we learned the first of many routines. Just like in the days before I discovered the Deaf world, I watched, lipread, and memorized the movements. I absorbed it all except for this one turn-and-kick combination. It was a combination that required us to execute a double-kick, followed by a full turn, and then some other fairly complicated movements. The owner was talking, cueing us along as she made the movements. Whenever she executed the turn, I would miss the cues for the next few movements because, while we were all turning, I could not lipread her. It all happened so fast, and I was losing heart by the minute every time we came to that turn. Although the routine only called for that movement a few times, I began to feel greatly discouraged.

When the evening was over, the owner came up and asked me how I was doing. I sadly shook my head and said, "I don't think I will be coming back tomorrow." She said, "Oh no! Come back. You did great!" I felt sufficiently encouraged, so I rallied, took her advice, and returned the next day. I thus made it through the first hurdle.

On Saturday, we were joined by the owner's entire cadre of instructors. To her credit, she probably had at least thirty working instructors in her company. Several of these instructors took turns teaching a routine to the rest of us.

The routines were all printed on sheets of paper that were given out prior to each training segment. The instructors would look at the papers, watch the trainer who was teaching the steps, and follow along, making notes. Specific segments of the popular songs they were using were associated with specific movements, making the task of memorization easier for the instructors. The group members were easily able to listen to the trainer while simultaneously looking at their papers and going through the movements of each routine several times.

I, however, had a distinct disadvantage in that there was no way I could look at the paper while listening to the trainer. I gave up using the papers and just concentrated on lipreading and watching the trainer. Fortunately, only a few of the routines had those blasted turns in them. And, my experience with the drums, knowledge of musical patterns (from a few years of piano lessons on Mead Avenue and a year of drum lessons at Cos Cob School), excellent memory, and talent for movement in general held me in good stead. With these skills, I made it through the second hurdle, having lasted through Saturday with confidence in the knowledge that I would be able to use the papers to later practice on my own to fully memorize those routines.

Auditions were held on Sunday. I was asked to do a particular routine, a slow one, a warm-up. I could not hear the music very well, and I was very nervous. To make matters worse, the owner had decided that this one instructor, who I learned I would apprentice with if I made it through the audition, should "help" me by clapping out the beat. For some reason, she decided to clap very slowly, on every other beat which was not helpful at all and was, in fact, quite maddening. It was another example of everyone knowing I was deaf but not knowing what to do about it! I knew at the time that I needed her to clap in a different way, to clap with every single beat. But who was I to tell her, this established instructor in the company I was trying to join? As has often been the case throughout my life, I was reluctant to advocate for myself.

Either the owner really wanted to hire me, or she had lots of pity for me, or my skills were obvious on Saturday because I don't know how they could have accepted me based on that audition. So I passed, and little did I know that I would have many other opportunities to advocate for myself down the road.

Next came my "apprenticeship," as they called it. I was assigned to work with that slow clapper I'd had difficulty with earlier. Although we taught a class on the Gallaudet campus together, this woman could not sign, and we didn't have an interpreter. But eventually, I passed this hurdle as well, and soon I was solely responsible for the classes at Gallaudet, teaching two of them twice a week.

I loved teaching those classes. They were full, and the students loved them. It was a great workout and it was fun, and here I was sharing my new love for exercise with people with whom I could communicate freely. My goal exactly.

Toward the end of my second year teaching these classes, a disconcerting thing happened. I was leading a routine, and in walked a woman that I knew only vaguely, the company owner's assistant. I never did learn exactly what her role was, but that day, she sat down over on the far side of the room and observed for the entire hour. I assumed that it was a standard evaluation observation and taught as usual. When the class was over, I went over to her and noticed that she had been making a list and drawing some illustrations on a notepad of the signs and visual cues I used for various movements.

I was a bit stunned, to say the least. I was well aware that the owner wanted to advertise the fact that her company had classes for deaf people. She had asked me to participate in some demonstrations around the area for this purpose, and I had willingly volunteered several times. But, now I was wondering what the purpose of the list could be.

I made an appointment to meet with the owner. Sure enough, she had her designs on compiling a book of signs for aerobics. I told her I thought it was a wonderful idea, and that I wanted to be in charge of the project. She said she was sorry, I could not be in charge of it, because the book was being overseen by my former apprenticeship supervisor, who could not sign, but who, as the owner explained, knew more about aerobics. But she would welcome my help.

I handed in my resignation papers to this company. To the owner's great credit, we bumped into each other at the local grocery store some years later, and she told me directly that she had made a mistake, and that she was very sorry. I thought that took both courage and insight.

A funny story, perhaps illustrating serendipity or blessings at their best, revolves around how I shortly thereafter managed to land a full-time job promoting exercise at Gallaudet University. I had been working in Dr. Merrill's office during the same few years that I had been teaching aerobics. When Dr. Merrill retired, the Board of Trustees hired Lloyd Johns as the new president of Gallaudet University. As Dr. Johns was hiring his own office staff, my position in the office was eliminated. However, he graciously met with me and asked me to name three departments or programs on campus where I thought I could contribute. By this time, I was very involved with exercise and had also determined that I would pursue a doctorate in either physical education or recreation. So naturally, my three choices included the Department of Physical Education and Recreation. A few days later, Ron Dreher, the chair of that department, walked into my office and asked me if I would like to coordinate the ongoing intramurals program and set up a new campus recreation program. Talk about something falling into your lap. Door closed, window opened.

From there, I plowed full steam ahead into what became a fifteen-year stint promoting exercise in the Deaf community. First, I hired some students to run the intramurals program. Then, I hired Sue Gill (now Sue Gill-Doleac) to help set up the campus recreation program with a focus on racquetball and aerobics. The Gallaudet Workout was launched with seven to eight instructors and 250 faculty, staff, and student participants. And I started documenting the visual cues we were using.

In the late 80s and early 90s, I spent many airborne hours flying to various cities in the United States, giving two kinds of workshops. I gave workshops for local d/Deaf individuals, educating them about the importance of fitness and teaching them the basics of aerobic exercise so that they could comfortably participate in classes at local clubs and recreation agencies. And, I would give workshops for the exercise instructors of those local clubs and agencies, training them in the "art of visual cueing," as I called it, as well as in the nuances of the Deaf community.

That was a fun job. I met many people, both deaf and hearing. I felt like I was making a real contribution by helping other d/Deaf people become aware of opportunities in the hearing world that they could take advantage of if they so desired. The many warmhearted group exercise instructors who attended my workshops were eager to learn. The club owners and managers who organized the workshops were generous hosts. They spent hours planning and marketing my workshops to the local instructors. Most of them also assisted in setting up the workshops for the local Deaf community as well. I remember many of these owners and managers fondly and with much gratitude for their support of my efforts.

There is a part of this story that from some perspectives should be left unsaid. However, to leave it unsaid would omit important evidence of the widespread attitudes toward d/Deaf people and toward sign language that continues to pervade our society.

There were and are a number of professional organizations for aerobics instructors. I attempted to become involved with these organizations by making presentations at national and international conventions. Many of the movers and shakers of that industry at that time became well aware of what I was trying to achieve. I lobbied the entire aerobics world to adopt as the industry standard the visual cues that were developed by me and my colleagues at Gallaudet so that they could be used in exercise classes all over the world. I wanted this to be an example of d/Deaf people giving back to the hearing world, to help erase the idea that d/Deaf people (and other "disability" groups) are always and ever the beneficiaries of services, rather than the providers. I wanted to demonstrate that d/Deaf people could provide a solution to a common problem, and that sign language could be of use to everyone.

Unfortunately, I was pigeonholed. The leaders of the industry decided that the visual cues developed by my colleagues and I were appropriate for d/Deaf people, but not appropriate for everyone else in the world. It was a matter of politics and personalities, not of substance at all. The cards were stacked against me. My goal was not attained.

Truthfully, I am sure I made some mistakes. During those frustrating years, I often thought that I needed to garner more support from the Deaf community. I engaged other d/Deaf women and men who wanted to become instructors. I helped them get involved and usually had several fellow d/Deaf people with me at the large industry conventions. I guess I only had enough energy for what I did do.

Looking back, it is obvious that I was an outsider trying to become an insider, and I faced extra barriers—my deafness and the hearing world's preconceived notions about d/Deaf people. It was hard, if not impossible, to rub elbows, network, and pick up the phone to chat. In the earlier years of this effort, I was honored with two very prestigious awards—the Christine MacIntyre Award from IDEA, the Association for Fitness Professionals, in 1988 and the Healthy American Fitness Leader Award (HAFL) in 1989. It was easy for them, I guess, to recognize my efforts in this formal way. It was hard, apparently impossible, however, for most of them to include me in

My headshot from the Healthy American Fitness Leaders program the year I was inducted.

their inner circle. I was functionally included, but not socially included, like so many solitaires in schools over the years and today.

I did meet many special people who became one-on-one friends. I miss them; we have been out of touch since my work in the industry fell by the wayside. Those friends reached out, sat with me, and tried to give support, and I remain grateful. Some of these folks were there for me steadily and intensely.

It was not all for naught. The job was challenging and never boring. I continue to meet people in the Deaf world who know me as the "aerobics woman." I especially loved training d/Deaf instructors and know that some of them are still teaching classes and promoting healthy lifestyles. The work kept me in great shape through my thirties and forties, allowed me to see much of the United States, and earned me numerous Frequent Flier miles. And, of course, the HAFL award led to my meeting Linda and Summer Crider. The wonderful people I met made it all worth it.

An Ongoing Foray Full of Grace And Truth: The Bethany Story

When I hit forty, I launched upon a spiritual search. Actually, it would be more accurate to say that I took my spiritual search off the back burner. Throughout my life, I would meet people who would talk about their churches, and out of curiosity, I would invite myself. I would go, but those particular churches didn't seem to have the combination of things I was looking for. Either the service was too long, too superficial, or too stuffy. I don't think I knew really what I was looking for; but when I found it, I knew.

I was still deeply mired in the aerobics world when I met Rena. She was in the audience at a conference where I was giving a presentation about how instructors and managers could market fitness programs to the Deaf community by employing d/Deaf individuals in various capacities. It was surely another serendipitous or divinely intentioned occasion. She was a therapeutic recreation specialist working for Easter Seals, and she had some grant money to set up "inclusion programs." She was also of Italian heritage and had grown up in an immigrant family, and we clicked from the start. She was very willing to help me in any way she could, and we set up some classes at the local YMCA and a private health club. She learned to sign, and we developed a role for her as my "hearing assistant." In a nutshell, she acted as an interpreter for my interactions with the hearing members of the classes, and she also helped me get back on the beat when I occasionally lost it. (Because these classes were based in local community centers and thus had more hearing than d/Deaf members, I couldn't crank up the music as loudly as I was accustomed.) We had several successful classes and became good friends simultaneously. Rena attended many industry conventions with me, including the awards ceremonies. She was my interpreter/supporter/hairdresser/make-up artist. I liked that! I think every successful d/Deaf woman needs such an assistant if her work involves forays into the solitary mainstream.

At some point along the way, Rena invited me to Bethany Community Church, which met in the local high school annex. Now, I thought that was probably on the odd side as churches go, but I prided myself on having an open mind. Rena said she would interpret for me. I figured it would be good practice for her.

As it happened, that Sunday, the pastor, Kevin McGhee, was beginning a series of sermons on marriage. Rather than calling it a sermon, however,

Kevin McGhee and his daughter Bryden chat with Rick and me at a Christmas event. Rick, myself, and others have built a model for inclusion at Bethany Community Church.

he referred to his talk as a "message." That, in itself, was impressive to me. That morning, his message was directed at husbands. He told them, in a nutshell, that they should be equal partners in maintaining the household and family ("don't wait to be *asked* to take out the trash, take it out already!") and that they should not even so much as *look* at another woman. I liked that! I thought, "This guy knows where it's at. I think I will go back again."

So back I went, first sporadically and then regularly. I liked Kevin's messages, and the music was nice. I was the only d/Deaf person there, so it was very much like being a solitaire again, alone at school. Except, this time, my one friend could sign.

One thing led to another, and after about a year, Rick, my husband-to-be, started to attend with me. Kevin performed our marriage several months later. Although we both really liked the messages and just about everything else about this church, we longed for more Deaf companionship. We couldn't get comfortable with being "alone in the mainstream" for church purposes.

We did some "church shopping" and discovered a Deaf church. Neither of us had ever been to a Deaf church. Going there was probably the closest either one of us got to attending a deaf school. Everyone there was deaf, including the pastor, the pastor's wife, all the leaders, and the attendees. We started taking turns going to Bethany and this Deaf church, and we attended a Bible study at the latter. Each church had things we liked, but both were lacking something. Bethany was lacking d/Deaf people and signers. The Deaf church lacked the more contemporary message we preferred.

As members of both churches would say, God had a plan. One day, Kevin asked to meet with Rick and me. Rena joined us as well. They asked us if we thought Bethany could meet our needs; they were aware that we were attending both churches and were sincerely concerned about our ability to get our spiritual needs met. We told them we would think about this. About a month later, we met again, and Rick and I shared our vision for a Deaf church like Bethany. In other words, we didn't want to be solitaires, but we wanted a Deaf church that had what Bethany had—the contemporary focus, great music, and some educational programs we thought were important.

That was 1993. Today, Bethany probably has one of the strongest Deaf ministries in the United States. It is not the only one, however, and I can only speak about Bethany (e.g., not about other integrated congregations). I would daresay that in faith-based organizations like Bethany, one will find the best model for inclusion, bringing deaf and hard of hearing people and hearing people together as equals.

The road to comfortable integration was not an easy one. In 1994, the church moved out of the high school and into an office/meeting space. In 1999, it acquired land and began building a home of its own (i.e., a "real church"). So, the early years of the Deaf ministry were actually the early years of the church as a whole. I feel that the ministry's survival is a testament to the patience and willingness of the hearing leaders as much as to the desires of a few persistent Deaf individuals. It was a novel experience for all of us. The hearing leaders had to learn about our needs. Rick and I received more practice than ever before in our lives in explaining (again and again) to hearing people what we needed (and why we needed it) in order to feel welcome and valued.

I tell this story for what it illustrates about how people can create the "ideal mainstream." Only the individuals involved can fashion it. It cannot be legislated by a government. Though the law says that deaf and hard of hearing children have the right to be physically in the same educational setting as hearing children in the tax-supported school system, we cannot mandate social interaction or acceptance. And while the law can say anything it wants about services in public recreation agencies, it apparently cannot force adults to take advantage of those services. In other words, we really cannot legislate inclusion in its essence, particularly not in settings that are voluntary, such as recreation centers and churches.

I have come to believe that for inclusion to take place in any setting, it must be desired by the people in that setting. It has to be chosen by individuals, both hearing and deaf. Bethany Community Church stands as an example of what can happen when hearing people *want* d/Deaf people in their midst in a way that is affirming for all. Integration begins when one or a few d/Deaf individuals see something they want and take the first step into the hearing environment, whether it be a church or a yoga class or a backpacking trip. The involvement of d/Deaf individuals will only be longstanding, however, if they see evidence of respect, affirmation, and willingness to modify programs as requested. The hearing individuals must accept that d/Deaf adults know best what works for them and for deaf children as well.

In those first few years, Rick, Rena, Kevin, and I embarked upon the task of building a Deaf ministry that would be attractive to d/Deaf adults. We were fortunate to acquire excellent volunteer interpreters, which is critical in such settings. Although public school children may suffer for years with less-than-qualified interpreters, deaf and hard of hearing adults will simply vacate the premises when faced with one. We were fortunate also that one of the first few Deaf attendees (i.e., me) was musically skilled and willing to do song interpretation. Bethany's service includes thirty minutes of music and thirty minutes of pastoral message. So, we needed both kinds of interpretation.

The Sunday morning service at Bethany provides a model of collaboration and equality of contribution. During the music portion of the service, a Deaf "singer" stands alongside the hearing musicians, and during the pastoral message, a hearing interpreter stands on the stage alongside the pastor. In the beginning, the interpretation team consisted of one Deaf and one hearing individual. The team quickly grew to include several hearing interpreters and several Deaf music translators. The oversight team (Kevin, Rena, Gina, and Rick) began with two hearing and two Deaf individuals, and today, consists of one hearing and four Deaf individuals.

Our coordinator, Bobby, is hearing, and we call him our "home grown" leader. We, the Deaf members, taught him to sign and about our culture and chose him to be our leader. His natural propensity for American Sign Language (ASL) and his willingness to be of service made him a godsend, literally. His story includes a lesson for everyone as well.

One day, Rick came home and told me that a guy from church named Bobby had approached him and wanted to know how and where he could learn to sign. Bobby's wife was on the road visiting family for six weeks, and Rick wondered if we could invite him over for dinner. "A hearing guy who wants to learn to sign?" I asked, with a knowing look. It is common for people to tell us they want to learn to sign; it is uncommon for them to actually invest their own time and money in this pursuit. Many give up after one class, feeling that it's too hard, they have no one to practice with, or some other reason. So, I had to be willing to once again see if someone was going to make good on their intentions.

So, over he came. I look back on Bobby's visit, and the many that followed during that year as lessons in patience. Bobby is the kind of guy who will laboriously try a new skill, regardless of how hard it is for him, or how slow he has to go, or how much he is taxing the patience of his teachers. All the patience (his and ours) was well worth it, because within two years, his signing skill was beyond all and any classes offered in the Washington, D.C.

area. This, in addition to his interest, skills, and education in ministry in general, made him a likely choice to lead the Deaf ministry. Bethany continues to explore how to locate and train d/Deaf individuals who can serve at this level and beyond. When we deliberated about the possibility of appointing Bobby to the leadership role, it was with full cognizance that eventually we would want a d/Deaf person in this role.

The Deaf leadership team at Bethany continues to spend energy seeking a balance between integrated activities and Deaf-only activities. We seek a balance between providing sign language interpreters for church-wide activities, such as the Sunday morning service, and ASL activities, such as weekly Bible study. We offer periodic sign language classes and "orientation to deafness" seminars for the hearing people. We host periodic open forums to discuss the issues and needs of our regular d/Deaf attendees. We in the Deaf ministry will argue with Bethany's hearing leaders if we feel that certain decisions or policies that impact the d/Deaf members are not "Deaf-friendly."

Crafting the music-filled first half of the Sunday morning service to meet the needs of d/Deaf individuals has been and remains problematic. Over my more than ten years of involvement, I have had much interaction with Kevin and the music leaders in my efforts to modify this thirty minutes into a pleasing and edifying experience for the majority of d/Deaf viewers who do not have the residual hearing to enjoy contemporary church music. It has been a struggle to craft services that will simultaneously meet the needs of d/Deaf and hearing attendees during the worship segment (with its six to eight songs). A real dilemma is that for a contemporary church like Bethany, keeping up with popular music is an important part of our worship efforts. Even a traditional church will vary its music repertoire to some degree for its members. For d/Deaf members, however, a song that is particularly pleasing to the ear, or is the hottest thing on Christian radio at the moment, could be a nightmare to translate into ASL. And if the translator cannot really convey the song's intricate message to the d/Deaf audience, what is the value of that song to them? Needless to say, this is a case where perhaps there is no solution that will completely satisfy the needs of both the d/Deaf and hearing members in an integrated setting. However, there is enough trust, respect, and even affection among Bethany's members to allow for disagreement and painstaking efforts to understand and seek even elusive solutions. It is a community venture; I would daresay it is a family venture.

Another area where full integration has been elusive is in the area of group scripture study. The fact is many d/Deaf adults struggle with reading due to their unfortunate unfamiliarity with the English language. Perhaps the cochlear implant will change this. If so, I will consider implants a truly worthy venture. The difficulty some d/Deaf people have with reading makes it hard to integrate d/Deaf and hearing individuals in the study of any scriptural text. Our solution to the problem has been to host a Deaf Bible study. It works. In fact, we have learned that reading together as a group and analyzing sentences helps many d/Deaf adults improve their reading skills. My experience in these studies has actually led me to use group reading in the classes I teach at Gallaudet.

On the other hand, we continue to learn ways that d/Deaf people can contribute to the congregation at large. Recently, Bethany embarked on an effort to revise a workbook used to provide a common foundation of Biblical information to new members. I volunteered to serve on the committee, as did one other Deaf individual. This was an exciting new venture for both of us. We serve on a general church committee with an interpreter and are engaged in a writing and editing task related to the church at large (and not just to the Deaf ministry). On this committee, we have been reminded that there are also hearing people for whom reading the Bible is no easy task. But more importantly, we learned that the drawings, graphics, and translation work that we did for the Deaf Bible study could be used to help hearing people understand the Bible as well.

Here is a group of hearing people willing to admit and accept that they, in fact, have something to learn and gain from association with people who are deaf. And that is an important attitude shift that could conceivably spread good will beyond the church walls into the community—to parents, teachers, and school children.

So what are the features that make Bethany an almost ideal model for inclusion?

1. The hearing leaders respect and accept each d/Deaf individual. There is no expectation that all d/Deaf individuals will be alike in skill, motivation, education level, reading ability, and so forth.
2. The hearing leaders seek the advice of d/Deaf individuals in designing programs and accessibility features for d/Deaf people; they place d/Deaf individuals in leadership roles related to the Deaf ministry.
3. The hearing interpreter and the Deaf music interpreters stand on the stage alongside the pastor and the hearing musicians. They are included during planning and rehearsal periods as well.
4. The Deaf ministry sponsors formal and informal weekly and monthly programs where the primary language used is ASL. Hearing signers are always welcome to these, and in certain situations, voice interpretation is provided upon request.
5. Deaf members are regularly invited to work alongside hearing members on various projects; they are also welcomed into leadership roles in tasks that involve both hearing and d/Deaf members. Thus, d/Deaf individuals have opportunities to contribute to the church as a whole, and not just to the Deaf ministry.
6. Sign language classes are offered to hearing members on a regular basis. A fee is charged and a Deaf instructor is paid for this service.

Transitory Forays and Those Not Yet Taken

In chapter 4, I related my experiences with disclosure at my high school reunion and during solitary travels. These represented shorter forays, so to speak, than the excursions into the fitness world and the world of Bethany Community Church. The transitory forays are important not only because they demonstrate how to make disclosure effective but also because they have been important to my overall life satisfaction. When the manner of disclosure enables real solutions for either the long or short run, forays back into the solitary mainstream can be enriching and enjoyable. I am glad that I took the bold step to put myself into each of these environments. By doing so, I broke the mold set by my father and discovered how I can enjoy the company of d/Deaf people as well as hearing people in certain settings and circumstances.

I still hope to return to Washington College one day in some capacity. Every year, I receive invitations to various events, and every year, I decide not to go. I have ventured into Chestertown on several occasions since my graduation in 1972. But generally, I just take solitary walks around the town and campus. I have never contacted the alumni office or made any effort to talk with anyone.

As I've described, my days at Washington College were a mixed bag. I had a few friends but still felt very alone. I loved the town and I loved the schoolwork. I was a somewhat normal college student in that I also loved partying on the weekends, but the weeknights always found me studying. When I think about my "social life" I have to put quotes around it because to call it a social life requires a stretch of the imagination. I had, as usual, a few good friends. In particular, two girls, Kathy and Judy, were my life-savers. We would take study breaks and chat, or we would walk up to the only shopping center in town or to the sub shop on Sundays, and we would spend dateless Saturday nights bemoaning our "datelessness." Really, they were great friends, and like Mary Ellen and Bettina, they made my solitary life more bearable.

Recently, however, I had an experience that has heightened my resolve to take that leap. In November 2002 on my birthday weekend, I had the good fortune to visit Washington College with a Deaf friend and her hearing daughter. The daughter was a high school senior, and Washington College was one of her options for the coming year. We traveled in separate cars, and I planned to arrive early to take my usual walk around the town near the river, to "prime" my nostalgic juices.

The walk was lovely, and when I stopped at Dunkin Donuts, I was surprised at how friendly the local folks were, most of whom looked like retirees. They all smiled at me. Surely they would have talked with me but I, as usual, busied myself with my coffee and a newspaper. I thought "Oh darn, I sure would like to talk to them. Oh well."

At the appointed time, I walked into the admissions office to meet my friend and her daughter. We had a considerable wait while the prospective student had her interview; we read magazines and chatted with the interpreter who had been hired for my friend. I never had an interpreter, not even once, at Washington College. Little did I know how this would affect me in the next few hours.

After the interview, a young sophomore woman led us on a tour of the campus. She led us to the bookstore and then the cafeteria where years ago I first spotted the signing soccer players. By then, the nostalgic juices were really flowing. We entered the library, and things started really rumbling in my head, heart, and stomach. I love libraries, and this one was no exception. It had been my refuge from my progressively more isolated predicament years ago.

Next was a classroom building, one that had been constructed after my time there. The guide began to talk about the relationship between faculty and students. "What's so great about Washington College," she said, "is that the faculty are so very involved with the students. On the first day of class, they put their phone numbers—even their *home* phone numbers— on the board and tell you to call them any time. They are always available to help you. It's great!" She conveyed this message repeatedly during the rest of the tour. And each time she reminded us of this faculty—student bond, my emotions churned.

For the first time in my life, I felt something I could honestly call regret—for relationships that never were, for missed opportunities, for a more "normal" undergraduate experience. It was like when I listened to Summer's valedictory speech, except that this time, I did not cry!

In the weeks that followed, I had an intense desire to return to Washington College and grab what I missed. I tried to think of ways to do so— maybe I could teach a class, take a class, give a lecture. I talked with some colleagues and even wrote a short proposal. Then I just decided to put it on the back burner. It seemed like the timing was not right; I started to feel like it just wasn't meant to be. Maybe it's still a work in progress. But knowing I have had other successful forays makes it easier to conceive of yet another.

9

Children of Our Hearts:

A Change in the Neighborhood

BRINGING this book to a close has been difficult. The story is not complete. I am struck again by the lack of connection between and among solitaires who have faced great struggles yet have never found the oasis of the Deaf community. I am struck by stories I have heard about solitaires that may never see the light of day unless some astute researcher or counselor chooses to give them a voice.

One Solitary Mainstream Project participant shared a very sad story indeed. He attended a small oral program in a neighborhood school during the early 1960s with several other deaf and hard of hearing children of varying ages. Parents would drive (sometimes long distances) to bring their children to this school each day. As at Rick's school, most of the day was spent on speech training, and parents were responsible teaching "normal" subject matter during the evenings and weekends. As the children were deemed "ready" (the participant didn't know what criteria the school used but was pretty sure it was based on speaking ability), they were mainstreamed as solitaires in the local school nearest to their respective homes.

He explained that the majority of his classmates have had miserable lives. Two have committed suicide. Several have serious drug problems. None of them, except for this one participant in my study, went to college, and the rest hold unskilled jobs or are unemployed.

Without more evidence, people can dismiss this story of failed inclusion as heresy. Or as an isolated case. Or as exaggerated. I don't think so. But finding such solitaires who are not successful will be a challenge for researchers, and who will be motivated for the task? It concerns me. Without information from such adults, the Solitary Mainstream Project is only partially complete. Those in my study, myself included, have been among the fortunate ones.

It concerns me also that the adults surrounding the many deaf children receiving cochlear implants will fail to consider that these children may very well have many of the same struggles as the participants of the Solitary Mainstream Project. A few years ago, I heard a conference presentation by a person involved in making decisions about whether children were good candidates for implants as well as evaluating implantee progress. A successful candidate or implantee, she explained, is one who "can be fully mainstreamed within three years." The goal of implantation, it seems to me, is moving deaf and hard of hearing children into the solitary mainstream.

I fully recognize the need to tackle the issue of deaf children's language acquisition. As a faculty member, I have worked with many college students who struggle with the English language. It always pains me when people blame the victim. Deaf children don't struggle with the English language because they are naturally deficient when it comes to learning English. All of the DODs who have perfect English are evidence of that. But sadly, many deaf and hard of hearing individuals are deficient in English because the adults around them never figured out how to meet their needs.

I hope that cochlear implants will help with spoken and written language acquisition. That, in itself, would make life so much easier for many deaf and hard of hearing individuals. But until the device is capable of making a child hear normally *in all manner of social situations,* I do not believe it will do away with the social isolation experienced by the large majority of solitaires and almost-solitaires.

So what do we need to do to effect a change in the neighborhoods and schools so that solitaires will no longer feel isolated? What can we do for these children of our hearts? To begin with, I will address what deaf and hard of hearing adults themselves need to do. Perhaps the proverbial buck stops with us.

The Role of Deaf and Hard of Hearing Adults

I had the very good fortune to "mentor" a hearing mother and her deaf daughter, Linda and Summer Crider. When I met them, Summer had recently received her implant, and I had to put aside any negative ideas I already held about the implants. Here were a mother and a daughter, a child of my heart, who were asking for my help, and more importantly, for my friendship. Summer is now nineteen years old, and she and her mom are counted within my close circle.

I recently asked Linda what she wished had been different during Summer's K–12 years. She said, "I wish that the fighting between the two factions had been nonexistent; I always felt like I was being pulled and that I had to take a side. And really, I didn't have to. Summer can be and is part of both worlds, and that message should have been there from the start."

All Deaf adults should have a "Summer" (i.e., a deaf child to mentor, nurture, and support).[1] Every Deaf adult should follow the example of Shelly Santamaria and avail themselves to local solitary deaf children.

I learned of Shelly's story from her brother Russ, who was a student of mine at Gallaudet. I taught him in an independent study format; his main assignment was to read and analyze a popular book about exemplary leadership. At the end of the semester, he made a presentation that was open to the student body, and it was at this presentation that I met his older sister Shelly. I told her that I had been intrigued by what Russ shared with me about their K–12 years and asked if we might meet for coffee. Meet we did, and she shared freely with me what I consider a painful but perhaps all-too-common story.

> I wish so badly that my mother could have seen Russ's presentation about leadership. It was so great! But you know what, I would have had to voice interpret for her because she can't understand him when he talks! But I would have been happy to do that just so she could know he is a smart guy and he made a great presentation!

It is so strange how we grew up in different educational environments. He went to the deaf school; and first, I was in a small mainstream program with other deaf kids, and later, I was a solitaire. For some reason, I think just because I was more patient with schooling than he was, I learned to speak reasonably clearly, while he did not.

In 1998, I took a teaching job (I had a BA in Special Education) in a deaf class. I was appalled at how horrible it was. There were kids from age five up to age thirteen, and the teacher had them do the SAME work for "language," which was having them work on their handwriting. It was terribly oppressive. That made me vow to become a teacher of the deaf and change things. So, in 1999, I decided to go to graduate school at Gallaudet. Little did I know how much my life would change there!

The main thing that happened is that I quickly realized two things. First, I realized how much I had been missing out of conversations in the hearing world. I loved being at Gallaudet and made many friends and just immersed myself in that Deaf community. Secondly, I realized with a sense of horror, how much worse it had been for my brother. Because he doesn't speak clearly, no one ever talks to him! At family gatherings, people come up to me and ask me this or that. . . . It's very basic stuff, but it allows me to feel a little bit included. But Russ has always been excluded. And now I understood this. My blinders were off so to speak; and for a while, I was so furious! How could they treat him that way? It made me so mad!

I could really understand the pain in this woman's story. She went on to explain how during her first year at Gallaudet, she went home for a large family celebration. At this celebration, she was keenly aware of feeling left out and saw how much worse it was for her brother. She couldn't stand it, and as much as she tried, she could not hide her great discomfort. Her mother asked, "What's wrong?" Shelly replied that it was nothing—she was fearful of ruining her grandfather's birthday party. Her mother was insistent, so Shelly excused herself and went outside, trying to get away from her mother. But her mother followed, continuing to question her. Finally, Shelly's dam broke loose, and she poured out her hurt and anger for years of neglect and for her mother's lack of sign language skill. Mother and daughter both cried buckets.

Today, Shelly has a protégé—a six-year-old deaf boy—with whom she plans to maintain an ongoing relationship. The boy's young mother is from Shelly's hometown and had the open-mindedness to seek out the counsel of a Deaf adult. She knew someone who knew someone, and now this mother regularly e-mails Shelly, and they visit when Shelly is back in her hometown. I was thrilled to hear this happy ending to a sad story, which has been too often repeated around the world. As in my relationship with Summer and her family, Shelly can be a guide for this family, helping them to learn of the Deaf community and all it can offer to their son.

You Have to Be Deaf to Understand

What is it like to "hear" a hand?
You have to be deaf to understand!
What is it like to be a small child,
In a school, in a room void of sound—
With a teacher who talks and talks and talks;
And then when she does come around to you,
She expects you to know what she's said?
You have to be deaf to understand.

Or the teacher thinks that to make you smart,
You must first learn how to talk with your voice;
So mumbo-jumbo with hands on your face
For hours and hours without patience or end,
Until out comes a faint resembling sound?
You have to be deaf to understand.

What is it like to be curious,
To thirst for knowledge you can call your own,
With an inner desire that's set on fire—
And you ask a brother, sister, or friend
Who looks in answer and says, "Never Mind"?
You have to be deaf to understand.

What it is like in a corner to stand,
Though there's nothing you've done really wrong,
Other than try to make use of your hands

To a silent peer to communicate
A thought that comes to your mind all at once?
You have to be deaf to understand.

What is it like to be shouted at
When one thinks that will help you to hear;
Or misunderstand the words of a friend
Who is trying to make a joke clear,
And you don't get the point because he's failed?
You have to be deaf to understand.

What is it like to be laughed in the face
When you try to repeat what is said;
Just to make sure that you've understood,
And you find that the words were misread—
And you want to cry out, "Please help me, friend"?
You have to be deaf to understand.

What is it like to have to depend
Upon one who can hear to phone a friend;
Or place a call to a business firm
And be forced to share what's personal, and,
Then find that your message wasn't made clear?
You have to be deaf to understand.

What is it like to be deaf and alone
In the company of those who can hear—
And you only guess as you go along,
For no one's there with a helping hand,
As you try to keep up with words and song?
You have to be deaf to understand.

What is it like on the road of life
To meet with a stranger who opens his mouth—
And speaks out a line at a rapid pace;
And you can't understand the look in his face
Because it is new and you're lost in the race?
You have to be deaf to understand.

What is it like to comprehend
Some nimble fingers that paint the scene,
And make you smile and feel serene,
With the "spoken word" of the moving hand
That makes you part of the word at large?
You have to be deaf to understand.

What is it like to "hear" a hand?
Yes, you have to be deaf to understand.

Madsen's poem, penned decades ago, declares that one must be deaf to understand what it is like to be deaf. I believe he was correct up to a point. Yes, every deaf solitaire or almost-solitaire needs at least one person in their lives who really understands how they experience the world. Generally, that would be a Deaf adult. This advocate/mentor/counselor/friend will teach others in that child's circle what they need to know in order to understand how to meet that child's needs. With this, one *won't* have to be deaf to understand.

Another way deaf and hard of hearing adults can become involved in the lives of solitaires is through the planning and promotion of recreational programs and activities that will bring solitaires together. With this critical mass of solitaires, the deaf and hard of hearing adults can plan activities that include hearing children also but that are designed with the deaf children's needs at the forefront.

Dwight and Beth Benedict are the parents of two girls—all four family members are deaf. It is little wonder that Dwight and Beth, both DODs, would take the lead in teaching the local parks and recreation agency and some area nonprofit organizations how best to include deaf children in recreational and leisure activities.

Beth and Dwight didn't do this alone; they had the support of other parents like themselves. In Montgomery and Frederick counties in Maryland, these Deaf parents volunteered their time to promote settings for their own deaf children so that they could benefit from public recreation resources *without* being solitaires. They enrolled their children en masse in summer camp programs sponsored by the local park and recreation agencies. Summer camp experiences planned in this manner ensure a critical mass of deaf children along with the hearing children who would normally participate.

Dwight also volunteered to coach sports teams that included his Deaf daughters and then recruited other deaf children to be on this same team. The net result was a team with both deaf and hearing children led by a Deaf coach. The park agency provided an interpreter in this situation, to assist communication between the Deaf coach and the hearing children as well as among the deaf children and the hearing children. Dwight and Beth also purchased a number of inexpensive sign language books to give out to the hearing children.

Why is this story so significant? Primarily because it illustrates how Deaf parents envision inclusion. Dwight and Beth wanted the number of deaf and hearing children on the team to be close to equal. They wanted the team to be coached by a Deaf person so that both groups of children (as well as the other parents involved and the parks and recreation staff members) could witness the leadership skills of a Deaf adult. This kind of experience, I believe, will change the views of the hearing people involved. It will destroy any preconceived notions they may have about of what Deaf adults and children are capable of.

Activities such as those planned by the Benedicts provide a rich sociological setting that begs for study. From such studies, we can learn about the intricacies of making leisure environments effective for both deaf and hearing children. It would be profitable to empirically examine how participation on a sports team made up of significant numbers of both deaf and hearing children could provide a valuable experience for all involved. The Deaf ministry at Bethany Community Church and the approach of Tom Holcomb's parents to his elementary school years are other examples of Deaf adults designing inclusion on their own terms. Such work needs to be analyzed and documented.

In all of these examples, we see how the ingenuity of Deaf adults, in the interests of their deaf children as well as themselves, can forge novel and exemplary approaches to inclusion. Programs resulting from these innovations can truly meet the leisure needs of deaf children while simultaneously providing a rich leisure experience for neighboring hearing children. This model, developed by Deaf adults for deaf children, enables community-based entities to fulfill their obligation to provide socially meaningful opportunities to all members of the greater community.

The Role of Hearing Adults

The controversy over how and where deaf and hard of hearing children should be educated continues. The push toward inclusion and the impact of widespread cochlear implantation are like a two-lane, high-speed, high-walled roadway to the unknown, with many exits along the way to yet other unknown destinations. Those who travel this highway are all pioneers: the deaf and hard of hearing children, their classmates, the parents, the teachers, the administrators, and the doctors.

Parents and doctors may hope that with cochlear implants, deaf children will no longer be deaf and therefore have no need for interaction with other deaf children, much less sign language. Research thus far suggests that implanted children will function on the level of hard of hearing children when they are actually using their implants.[2] During elementary school, I had a 50-dB hearing loss, which is moderate by most standards, and I was an expert lipreader; however, this loss was enough to stand as a barrier between me and the very large majority of my classmates.

The sixty adults who shared their stories for this book said that their solitary mainstream experiences "made them who they are." However, they also shared hope that today's solitaires might "shed less tears" than they did. While they do not recommend a wholesale return to the days when all deaf and hard of hearing children attended residential or day programs, most of them temper their support of inclusion and cochlear implants with their own ideas of what is needed to make inclusion work. They are aware (often painfully aware) that being a solitaire in a hearing school (i.e., being the "beneficiary" of the inclusion philosophy) does not automatically make one accepted by others, create a healthy self-esteem, or offer the opportunity to develop one's full potential.

So what can be done to make inclusion all that we might imagine it to be in its ideal?

Perhaps the most all-encompassing recommendation from project participants is that parents and family members need to understand as much as possible about deafness, Deaf culture, the solitary life, assistive devices and strategies, sign language, and so forth. They need to accept that the child is deaf or hard of hearing and will always be so. They need to instill a healthy self-esteem, find ways to focus on the child's abilities, find ways to help him or her learn "practical tools for living as deaf person," and, in general, be as encouraging as they would with a hearing child.

Unfortunately, there are no enforceable laws or even guidelines about *who* should provide this information, to either the parents or to the teachers, coaches, and classmates. Thus, any adult—parent, teacher, coach, or school administrator—can decide to learn about these issues and initiate workshops, in-service training, and informal gatherings to promote Deaf awareness. Is it not the job of adults to do this? Several participants mentioned that they felt that everyone thought this "educating about hearing loss" was the child's job.

> In my growing-up years, I felt (and still feel, upon looking back) that virtually all the responsibility was mine. This should be avoided. Perhaps others (such as the interpreter, the IEP manager, school counselor, and even teachers) can be more actively involved in educating others through workshops, discussions, and activities. I consider it best to avoid putting all the expectations on the respective deaf student to do all the disclosing and educating. Why should a child be expected to do that? M 93

What should be included in such workshops and training programs? The solitary mainstream participants also mentioned a number of topics that should be discussed in Deaf awareness workshops:

- Causes and nature of hearing loss; issues of speech discrimination, residual hearing, hearing aids, and implants
- The history of deaf education, the Deaf community, sign language, oralism, and the accomplishments of Deaf individuals
- Activities offered by and within the Deaf community, including sports, festivals, community service, religious activities, and regular social gatherings

- Sign language interpretation (especially in the school setting)
- Assistive technology, including implants, hearing aids, closed captions, TDDs, pagers, e-mail, and instant messaging
- Different educational settings (residential schools, mainstream programs, inclusion), the social isolation often associated with inclusion and how it can be remedied, and the importance of extracurricular activities in developing friendships and self-esteem
- The importance of and issues surrounding informal conversation settings, such as the lunchroom, hallway, and locker room; why these settings are particularly difficult for deaf and hard of hearing children; and how these settings can be modified to address this, such as providing alternative quiet places for the children to eat lunch
- How teachers can modify classroom activities to make them easier for deaf or hard of hearing children, such as using small group or partner discussions versus whole class discussions, repeating students' questions and important points, enunciating clearly and requiring students to do the same, having speaking students stand at the front of the room, providing good seating and adequate light, not talking to the blackboard, and so forth.

In addition to such workshops, there is a need for sign language classes. According to the *2001–2002 Annual Survey of Deaf and Hard of Hearing Children and Youth*, only 12 to 13 percent of the families of solitaires and almost-solitaires use sign language. I am always saddened on graduation day at Gallaudet, because I am reminded how few families learn to sign. I dread watching the graduates and their families have strained or limited conversations. Seeing a student who loves to talk and talks well in sign struggle to speak verbally to parents disheartens me. Speaking verbally is probably the thing these students do least well, and witnessing such poor communication convinces me that surely those hearing parents have limited knowledge of what their son or daughter could really talk about if allowed to use the language they know and use fluently.

The Role of at Least One Knowledgeable Adult

Deaf or hard of hearing solitaires must have at least one knowledgeable adult, preferably deaf or hard of hearing as well, with whom they can talk on a frequent basis about whatever issues arise. Such an adult can provide a safe space for deaf or hard of hearing children to explore their feelings about day-to-day experiences with teachers and classmates.

> In my high school years, I had a counselor. . . . She was really an elementary school teacher who knew sign language and was the first teacher in the mainstreamed program that started in the elementary school and grew as the kids grew older. They told her about me at the high school, and she would start coming over once a week to meet with me and make sure my needs were being met at school. I looked forward to seeing her, as we would talk about different things. My deafness was a safe topic to talk with her about because she understood. She taught sign language classes, and my mother and I signed up together. They were a lot of fun. She also introduced me to Gallaudet, and I have much to thank her for.   F 90

The phenomenon of talking about experiences of frustration or even oppression is common in minority groups. Beverly Daniel Tatum explains how black adolescents become aware of this need to share stories with persons whom they have reason to believe will genuinely empathize.[3] At this age they realize that if they confide to a white classmate about perceived racist remarks by a teacher, the white student is likely to attempt to assure the black student that the teacher "was just kidding." If, however, the black student describes the racist remark to a black classmate, that classmate is more likely to affirm and/or empathize with the feelings evoked by the remark. A deaf solitaire needs to have easy access to at least one person who can truly understand her situation, so that when difficult issues arise (and they will), she will feel that this person *will* affirm and empathize with her feelings.

One role for this knowledgeable adult, which I feel is critical, is that of observer. Claire Ramsey was able to make observations and write her eye-opening book, *Deaf Children in Public Schools*, precisely because she sat in those classrooms for a year. Because she is fluent in sign language, she was able to make sense out of the communication among the deaf and hearing classmates. Only an observer fluent in sign language could have done this.

I know it would be quite difficult for someone to observe a solitaire for a full year, but to have someone observe one day a week would not be an unreasonable expectation. If I were the parent of a deaf child and I wanted her to attend the neighborhood school, I would do just that. Or I would obtain the services of a knowledgeable adult (someone who knows sign language, knows the issues deaf and hard of hearing children face in mainstream settings, and so forth) to do this observing. Knowing what we know from adults who have been there, every solitaire deserves to have an adult observing his or her school day on a regular basis until it is determined that no further modifications are necessary. To lessen the obtrusion, the observer could volunteer as a classroom helper.

There is no way parents can really know what is going on with their deaf child unless such observations are regular and commonplace. With such information, a parent is in the best position possible to make recommendations and choices about the child's schooling. As one of the solitary mainstream participants so aptly put it, this would be the closest a hearing adult could get to actually experiencing what the child is experiencing.

> I wish those people making decisions about special education could see how deaf students truly function in the mainstream before deciding that as many deaf children as possible should be mainstreamed. Better still, I wish they could experience the isolation firsthand, as I bet they would quickly change their minds and see the wisdom in paying the extra money to educate deaf children in signing environments where there is more equal access to communication. Parents need to educate state representatives and school officials about the tremendous price that deaf children pay socially and in terms of self-esteem in the mainstream environment. F 83

Lessons from the Field of Leisure Studies

For both children and adults, most life satisfaction comes from leisure. And most leisure choices involve other people. We do fun things with other people, be they family or friends. While we do these fun things, we talk. We converse. We share; laugh; commiserate about our jobs, kids, in-laws, the state of the world; and talk about our latest acquisitions, be they stocks, sheets, snowboards, or speedboats.

Our leisure time, like our extracurricular activities during our K–12 years, is the major life area over which we can exercise a significant degree of control. Most parents are very concerned about their child's life satisfaction (commonly known as happiness). Soccer moms and baseball dads are entrenched features of our culture. Moms and dads make cookies for class parties, serve as scoutmasters, drive kids to events, and sit in a "parents' room" while the kids do their thing. Most parents' lives revolve around their children's fun (i.e., leisure activities).

What of deaf or hard of hearing children who are mainstreamed as solitaires? How does their involvement in leisure activities, and thereby their life satisfaction, evolve? How does their K–12 experience prepare them for adult choices? What choices do they make, as adults, for their life satisfaction?

As described in chapter 4, the solitary mainstream participants emphasized repeatedly in their writings how unsatisfying their extracurricular activities were in their K–12 years. In essence, they expressed dissatisfaction with the quality of *social interaction within the extracurricular activity.* They recognized that these activities provide a structured environment within which friendships can be developed around common interests and thus could and should provide an arena for the solitaire to more easily interact. In chapter 6, we saw that a crucial element of their adult lives, a crucial element of leisure and thereby life satisfaction, revolves around who they chose to interact with—Deaf people, hearing people, signers, non-signers. Simply put, who they choose to interact with will impact the quality of conversation during leisure time.

Douglas Kleiber, chairperson of the Department of Leisure Studies at the University of Georgia, speaks of "the fourth environment," represented by the tendency of adults to congregate in a coffee shop or a bar, on some regular basis, "just to talk." Adolescents do this also—in malls, on street corners, and in other uniquely designated venues. This fourth environment is defined as "beyond home, school, or work" and is a place for people to discuss things and make sense of what is happening in their lives. For adolescents in particular, an important element of these environments is the *absence of adults*.

> The social tasks of adolescence and early adulthood may benefit more from unstructured leisure contexts since there is more influence over communication and interaction patterns in those situations than when adults are in control. Adolescents in search of companionship and/or romance seek out such fourth environment contexts as shopping malls, house parties, coffee shops, and swimming pools. And even when children's activities are organized and structured by adults, informal child-centered interaction is likely to persist as a part of the experience.[4]

Adults lament how easy it is to forget the throes of late childhood and adolescence. We think of today's adolescents as being much more rebellious than we were. We certainly would recall, however, that as teens we wanted to be away from adults. For deaf adolescents, how will they participate in this fourth environment? Would an interpreter help?

> I was lucky in that my speech was so understandable and that I could interact with my peers as well as I did, but I am sure that other deaf kids thrown into mainstream situations with even more communication barriers than I had struggled even more, particularly if they used an interpreter. An interpreter is all well and good for the "formal" kind of classroom communication, but an interpreter is an adult and an artificial third party in the communication between deaf kids and their hearing peers. Deaf kids miss out on informal chatter between their classmates because (1) the interpreter can't or doesn't want to interpret it all; and (2) because the interpreter's very presence creates a psychological barrier between a deaf student and his or her classmates that precludes the informal chitchat.   F 83

Lessons from the Media

Recently, a young Deaf woman named Christy Smith was a contestant on the reality TV series *Survivor.* I watched almost every episode, hoping she would win. Every week, I would check on America Online to see how she was rated (I would never have watched *Survivor,* let alone check the popularity ratings on AOL, if it weren't for her) and was pleased to see that people were indeed impressed by her. But, by far, the most important aspect to me about this entire experience is that millions of people got to observe, just as Claire Ramsey had, the daily life of a solitaire.

Christy's father learned new things about his daughter from watching her interact with the other people on the show. He cried because he realized that prior to watching the show, he had no idea just how frustrating things could be for his daughter.[5] At one of her first public appearances after leaving the show, Christy credited her experience at the Model Secondary School for the Deaf on the Gallaudet University campus, for giving her an identity, confidence, and a positive outlook on life.[6]

For me, the most memorable segment of the show was when Christy and another contestant each received and read a letter from a loved one. Christy read her letter and cried alone. The other contestant (the one who actually won this particular series) read her letter while her best friend on the show hugged her and wept with her. Stark contrast, I thought. Such is frequently the lot of a solitaire, to cry alone.

We Should Expect More of the Same Until Proven Otherwise

For the sake of children in school today and tomorrow, we should assume that the solitary mainstream experience has not changed. Until cochlear implants make it possible to easily chat in lunchrooms, hallways, bleachers, locker rooms, college pubs, and snack bars, the social difficulties will remain. Until implants allow students to be privy to banter wherever it exists, they will not solve the dilemma faced by the solitary mainstreamed child, youth, or adult.

And thus,

- We must try to improve the social experience of solitary deaf children. The only way to do this is to change the knowledge base and the attitudes of everyone in their circle.
- We must accept that it is very difficult for persons who can hear to fathom the life of a deaf or hard of hearing person. This difficulty is exacerbated by the pervasive lack of awareness that Deaf people can be healthy, vibrant, and contributing members of society.

- Parents and teachers must learn and then impart to children, both deaf and hearing, as much information as possible about Deaf history and Deaf culture.
- Parents and teachers must learn to see each deaf and hard of hearing child as unique, special, and whole. At the same time, they must not put the child on a pedestal and must not teach that this particular child is better than all other deaf children.
- Parents must be open to the value of the Deaf community and signed languages and seek involvement with other families with deaf children and Deaf adults. The entire family should feel positive about the opportunity to be involved with two social worlds. The parents need to convey enthusiasm for meeting other families with a deaf member, meeting Deaf adults, learning sign, and having a whole new world opened up to them.
- Parents and teachers must understand the child's need to contribute, be needed, and be seen as a valuable member of his peer group. They must find ways to teach the deaf and hard of hearing child how hearing children interact, what they talk about, and how to comfortably enter established social circles.
- Parents and teachers must carefully observe (or enlist others to observe) the interactions among deaf and hard of hearing children and their hearing peers, and they should take steps to remedy unhealthy interaction patterns.
- Deaf and hard of hearing children and their peers must learn that deafness is not unique to this individual child. Deafness is common, and the issues faced by various Deaf people are similar regardless of where they live.
- Parents and teachers must accept that the people best able to teach about deaf and hard of hearing children are deaf and hard of hearing adults who are self-aware and willing to invest mentoring time with the family.
- Deaf and hard of hearing adults must accept responsibility for becoming self-aware so that they may be excellent mentors for hearing families with deaf children. They must recognize that this is an important

avenue in their quest for recognition as well as for the survival of the Deaf community.

- Parents and teachers must accept that when a solitaire fails, it is highly likely that the child could do better in a different school setting. Typical classrooms generally lack support for the unique needs of a deaf and hard of hearing child. Adults must look for system deficiencies before assuming it is the child's lack of knowledge, skills, or motivation.
- School systems and community systems (recreation services, social services) must take an active role by encouraging and supporting deaf and hard of hearing children and their families. They should provide leadership and support interaction between families with deaf members in the community. This should be an extension of attention to the needs of minority individuals and of efforts to embrace and nurture diversity.

Although the above recommendations may look like a tall order, we need to realize that such changes are necessary for deaf and hard of hearing children to achieve full inclusion. The more that families with solitaires seek to connect with each other and with the Deaf community, the less alone they will feel in their efforts. Ultimately, changes in attitudes and behavior will result in an end to the experience of surprise, anger, and puzzlement felt by solitaires upon meeting other Deaf individuals for the first time. These changes will result in an end to the isolation experienced by deaf and hard of hearing children. And they will prevent families from being beset with sad deathbed experiences, such as the one described below.

My father resisted all efforts to convince him to learn to sign. But actually, he did learn one sign. He learned the universal sign I LOVE YOU, or as Summer would call it, the SEE YOU LATER sign. My father signed this to me as I was leaving his hospital room at the Stamford Rehabilitation Center, where he was recovering from the first of two major strokes. This was the last time I saw him awake.

I saw him next after he'd had the second stroke, the one from which he did not recover. In his hospital room, I became aware of yet another disadvantage for a family who never learns to sign.

Dad appeared to be sleeping or in a coma. The doctors could not tell us whether or not he was aware of anything. "He might be; we just don't know," they said. I looked at him and noticed that his eyes seemed to be at least partially open. However, his head was facing down to the side of the pillow as if he could not move his head. I went over to that side of his bed, and crouched down to look up into his eyes. I put one hand over his and used my other hand to sign I LOVE YOU to him. He rolled his eyes. I felt that he saw me. I waved I LOVE YOU again, and he rolled his eyes again. I felt that maybe he still had awareness and knew I was there. As for my siblings and my mother, he would have been totally unaware of their presence, because no one else moved into his line of sight. He had a 100-dB loss, and wasn't wearing his hearing aid. There is no way he would have known of their presence through the sense of hearing. They reasoned that he probably didn't know I was there, that his eye-rolling was probably just a reflex. We will never know. But one thing I do know is that if Dad had set the example for us to learn sign and be more conscious of the Deaf individual's needs, they would have made an effort to communicate with him visually during possibly his last conscious hours.

So think about this. Here is a family with a Deaf member. No one knows how to sign. The Deaf member becomes seriously ill or injured. Will the hospital staff and family members always be careful to put on the Deaf individual's hearing aid or cochlear implant? Will they remember to shut off the air conditioner and other machines that are maddeningly humming in the background? And what about the fact that hearing aids and cochlear implants are imperfect? What about the fact that the individual thusly fitted still must lipread, and often with great effort? Will the hospital staff and family members still expect this ill or injured Deaf person to make this effort? Imagine trying to muster the strength to get well or face death in such an environment, where one is shut out from surrounding conversation.

I have made my plea. I hope those who need to will listen before it is too late. It was too late for my father. It's not too late for you.

Appendix

Research Methodology

I DETERMINED that the primary goal of my work would be to give voice to adults who had been the only deaf or hard of hearing child in their school for most of their K–12 years. Since I was concerned with finding in-depth information regarding the unique experience of a certain category of individual, I chose to do a phenomenological study.

Phenomenology, as its name suggests, is the study of human phenomenon. A phenomenological study is one that asks, "What was that experience like for that person or group of persons?" "How would that person describe his or her experience?" Books based on interviews with certain groups of people (e.g., holocaust survivors, women over fifty, or Vietnam veterans) are reflections of phenomenological inquiry. The researcher is not looking for any cause/effect relationship, but rather attempts to tell the story of the people who have lived with or through a certain experience or set of circumstances.

Search for Participants

Data collection for the Solitary Mainstream Project began in February 2000 when I posted an Internet notice on USA-L News, a private e-mail subscription list focusing on news items of interest for deaf or hard of hearing people. Several other deafness-related Web presences subsequently alerted their readers to this research opportunity.

In addition to this Internet posting, I sent letters to the coordinators of the deaf and disabled student services providers listed in the *College and Career Guide for Deaf Students*. Finally, letters were also mailed to past participants of Gallaudet University's New Signer's Program, a two-week program for incoming freshman.

Approximately 140 people responded, mostly in response to the Internet postings. These individuals were then sent additional information about the project and a demographic questionnaire designed to ensure that they met certain qualifications for inclusion in the study. I had previously determined that the informants would need to have been solitaires for at least seven of their K–12 years, have had at least a 50-decibel loss in both ears prior to age seven, and have graduated from high school in 1995 or earlier in order for them to have some perspective on the experience.

In addition to the demographic questions, the screening survey also included the following optional essay exercise:

> Please write a short (or long, if you like) essay describing the reasons why you would like to be included in this research project. Feel free to share anything you would like about your experience as the only deaf or hard of hearing child in your mainstream school. Feel free to include your suggestions for children who are currently mainstreamed.

This exercise was purposely global. I expected that their responses would provide some common themes whereby more specific essay questions could be developed.

More than 100 respondents chose to respond to this essay question; many wrote quite profusely. Their essays illustrated their eagerness to share their stories and a pervasive concern for today's solitaires.

The essays were analyzed with Ethonograph, a software program designed specifically for this kind of study. From the themes that emerged from the initial global essay, I composed four essay prompts to solicit more specific information.

To ensure that the themes identified were comprehensive, I shared them with peer reviewer Ms. Brenda Battat, then acting executive director of Self-Help for Hard of Hearing, Inc., and a graduate assistant, Ms.

Christina Shen. Ms. Battat did indeed identify a theme that I did not (disclosure), and I chose to include it in the investigation.

Sixty of the 125 original respondents agreed to participate in the full study. They completed four essays and a multiple-choice questionnaire during the summer of 2000.

The Four Essay Prompts

For Chapter 3

Tell me about the worst and best experiences you had with a teacher and with a fellow student. Please describe in as much detail as possible exactly what happened and why it was so awful or so great.

For Chapter 4

Tell me about how often (or how rarely) you "disclosed" your hearing loss to others in the school. To teachers? To peers? To a counselor? What was that like? How often did you talk with someone about your hearing loss and/or related needs? How did others respond to your sharing? This could range from reminding peers "remember I can't hear you when you are all talking at the same time" to talking with your counselor for an hour every week about the issues you were facing. Did you talk to parents or siblings about issues related to your hearing loss, and if so, how often? Try to give me the breadth and depth of your experience focused on this (talking to others about your deafness/hard of hearingness), even if it's just to say, "I never talked to anyone about my hearing loss, and here's why."

Do you think the amount of or quality of "talking about my hearing loss" with others was optimal (just perfect, not enough, not deep enough, whatever)? Can you think of anything that could have made it better for you? What can parents and schools do to help today's children with regards to addressing their loss and their needs in the solitary mainstream environment?

For Chapter 5

Many participants mentioned a strong academic experience juxtaposed with an unsatisfactory social experience (few friends, always left out of conversation and play, etc.). Some said that the strong academic skills gained were "worth the price," and some felt that the great social isolation significantly defeated the academic benefits.

A few described a positive social environment where they had a good number of hearing friends, felt accepted, and were involved in many activities. Sometimes, but not always, these participants had been educated in private or religion-based schools. Many mention "compensating" by finding their strengths and working very hard to excel in that area. Some proudly said, "It made me who I am," (with "it" referring to the solitary mainstream experience).

On the contrary, some participants described having had very unhappy and lonely school experiences. "I was very much a loner . . . had minimal social experiences. . . . I did not know where I belonged and struggled with depression and self-esteem. My relationships were all with adults, and I wanted peers to have fun with" were some of their comments.

Please give this juxtaposition your thoughtful consideration. In particular, what do you think makes it possible for some solitary mainstreamed children/youth to have a good social life? Why is there such a stark difference between a few participants who say their social experiences were enriching and satisfying, while others said it was unsatisfactory or even downright awful? What could be done to improve the solitary mainstream experience in this regard by the parents, by the schools, and by the children/youth themselves?

For Chapter 6

About half of you mentioned that you were thrilled to meet other deaf and hard of hearing children or adults in your K–12 or college years, and wish you had met them earlier in your life. At the same time, many of you mentioned being "afraid of" or "uncomfortable being around" other deaf and hard of hearing children/adults when you were younger. First, talk about this with regard to yourself. In particular, try to explain why you were "uncomfortable" or "thrilled" to meet other deaf and hard of hearing children.

Then, talk about today, in your adult life: How do you spend your leisure/social time? Describe your leisure/social involvement with other deaf and hard of hearing persons (spouse, friends, children, whatever). Also, describe your leisure/social involvement with hearing adults and/or children. Feel free to also mention leisure/social time spent alone if you feel that is significant.

Briefly tell me if you are satisfied with your current leisure/social life, and if not, what changes would you like to see?

Participant Characteristics

Project participants were from all over the United States and Canada, mostly white, more female than male, and ranged in age from twenty-eight to sixty-five. More significant than their age, perhaps, is the year they graduated from high school. This is important because it tells us the length of time they were in school after the implementation of P.L. 94–142, the Education for all Handicapped Children Act.

Twenty-two of the Solitary Mainstream Project participants graduated from high school between 1986 and 1995, and thus their school years were essentially within the period fully affected by this legislation. Another seventeen graduated between 1981 and 1985, and thus approximately half of their K–12 years occurred after this law's passage. The remaining twenty-one graduated prior to 1980 and thus were essentially educated before the mainstreaming era.

More than half of the informants were alone for their entire K–12 years. Others were alone for at least seven of those years. Slightly more than half were deaf from birth and had a profound hearing loss. Most of the remainder were prelingually deaf (prior to age three) and had a severe hearing loss. They attended rural, urban, and suburban schools.

Informants were asked to indicate the number of years they received certain support services. Speech therapy, tutoring, note-taking, interpreters, computer-assisted transcription, sign language classes, and planned activities with other deaf and hard of hearing children were included on the checklist. By far, the most prevalently provided service was speech therapy, with 20 percent of the informants receiving these services for their entire K–12 careers. Another 20 percent received these services for four to nine years. All other services were enjoyed by only a handful of informants. Only five of the participants ever had a sign language interpreter. More than half never had a tutor or a note taker. Those who did have a tutor or note taker had such support for only a few years.

In their adult lives, more than half of these individuals learned sign language and used it on a daily basis. Another 20 percent know some sign but do not have ample opportunity to use it—most of these express a wish for more contact with other deaf and hard of hearing individuals. Only eight have remained fully oral, fully immersed in the hearing world, with no contact with other deaf and hard of hearing people.

Limitations of the Study

In general, the findings of qualitative studies are considered not generalizable. From a pure research perspective, I cannot say that my findings show that all or most deaf and hard of hearing children who are mainstreamed as solitaires will have similar experiences. However, the essays echo substance from other scholarly reports and provide information helpful in understanding the solitary mainstream experience in general.

Although a college degree was not stipulated or implied as a requirement for participation, all but one of the informants are, in fact, college graduates. Approximately one-third graduated from Gallaudet University, a handful graduated from the National Technical Institute of the Deaf or California State University at Northridge, and the remaining two-thirds graduated from mainstream colleges and universities. The fact that the participants were a relatively educated group may simply reflect the fact that such people are more likely to have computers. They were in the habit of using e-mail regularly and were willing (and able) to reflect upon and write about their experiences. Surely there are adults who were mainstreamed as solitaires, who perhaps did not have as much academic success, whose voices are not represented herein.

The fact that twenty-one of the sixty informants graduated from high school prior to 1980 warrants additional comment. A perusal of essays submitted by this older one-third indicates that they faced issues and had experiences similar to those of the younger people. Some might argue that by virtue of P.L. 94–142 and other societal changes, the older group's school experience must have been different. However, conversations with professionals who work with current solitaires as well as recent studies suggest that the solitary mainstream experience continues to involve similar themes to those raised by the older informants of this study.

In the final analysis, this study does not answer the question "Is the solitary mainstream experience better today?" It does, however, provide us with information to keep in mind when we observe and investigate the experiences of current solitaires.

I purposely excluded Deaf of Deaf informants because I felt their perceptions of their solitary experience could be materially different from those deaf individuals born into hearing families. Finally, none of the volunteers had cochlear implants during their K–12 years.

Notes

Introduction

1. A person can have a mild, moderate, severe, or profound loss as measured by a series of hearing tests. These labels are often defined in terms of how they impact the ability to hear speech.

> Mild—difficulty hearing faint or distant speech, even in quiet environments;
> Moderate—hears conversational speech only at a close distance;
> Severe—cannot hear conversational speech;
> Profound—may hear loud sounds; hearing is not the primary communication channel.
> From B. Stach, *Clinical Audiology: An Introduction* (San Diego: Singular, 1998).

Hearing loss is generally described in terms of (1) how loud a pure tone needs to be for a person to clearly and consistently detect it and (2) the percentage of single- and two-syllable words a person will hear correctly when they are spoken at that loudness level (e.g., when they are "aided"). Tests for the spoken word yield a speech discrimination score. For example, Jane could have a 100-dB loss and a speech discrimination score of 32 percent. Robert may have a 50-dB loss and a speech discrimination score of 85 percent. Peter may have a 60-dB loss and a speech discrimination score of 45 percent. The speech discrimination scores refer to the percentage of words heard correctly during tests designed specifically to measure this ability. These scores will translate into deaf or hard of hearing children's ability to engage in conversation with their peers. An additional factor that greatly influences the lives of deaf and hard of hearing people is the age of onset, which refers to the age at which a person acquires a hearing loss. Generally speaking, if a child is born with or sustains a loss of hearing prior to age three, he or she will not acquire language in the effortless way that most people do. The child will require some kind of intervention or unusual measures to learn the spoken language of her (presumably hearing) parents. Rather than acquiring language by virtue of immersion in the home environment, she will have to be *taught* the language in some systematic way. An exception to this rule lies within Deaf children of Deaf families. Children in those families generally learn the native sign language first, and research has shown this language to be functionally equivalent to the spoken language, assuming a general level of education within the parents. These exceptions are evident not only in the United States but in European countries as well. When a child's parents are Deaf or are fluent in a sign language, the child learns that sign language as a native language without any unusual measures. In other words, if the child is surrounded by sign language, just as most children are surrounded by spoken language, he or she will acquire that sign language as a first language at the same rate as a hearing child would acquire his or her native spoken language. And the advent of "baby signs" for hearing children illustrates that infants actually will sign before they talk if they are exposed to signing consistently.

2. In his 1972 article, "Implications for Sociolinguistic Research among the Deaf," James Woodward proposed that the capitalized term *Deaf* be used to refer to Deaf people who share a language and a culture, and that the lowercase *deaf* refer to the audiological condition. As such, *Deaf* does not imply any specific degree of hearing loss. People can be audiologically hard of hearing and still think of themselves as Deaf as pointed out by Carol Padden and Tom Humphries in *Deaf in America: Voices from a Culture* (Cambridge: Harvard University Press, 1988).

I wish to respect this convention. In the case of the sixty individuals who shared their stories with me, a great majority made the choice to learn sign language and to avail themselves of the benefits of the Deaf community in early adulthood. Because of this, I determined that I could safely use the uppercase term when referring to them as well. In a few cases, where I quote another source or explain another person's point of view, if that person did not or would not use this convention, then I use the lowercase as such. Throughout the book I also use *d/Deaf* when I wish to refer to all people who have a significant loss of hearing—to include both those who think of themselves as Deaf and those who think of themselves as deaf, hard of hearing, or hearing impaired. Often, it was a judgment call, and I can only express that I have no wish to offend anyone by these judgments.

3. When I first embarked upon the research that culminated with this book, I pondered what to call "us"—people like me who were the only deaf or hard of hearing child in their school. I thought of "aloners," "loners," "only-ones," and a few others I cannot remember. *Solitary* was the label I initially settled on, after talking with some colleagues and also with those who had agreed to participate in

my research study. Then I thought it would be good to include a dictionary definition, since I was concerned that the "inclusion" advocates would take exception to this moniker we chose to apply to ourselves.

Lo and behold, in *Webster's*, I learned of the definition of *solitaire*. And I thought, how fitting. To me, the deaf and hard of hearing children are gems, alone but "as diamonds set in a ring." So that is what I ultimately decided to label us and them.

4. John V. Van Cleve, ed., *Deaf History Unveiled: Interpretations from the New Scholarship* (Washington, D.C.: Gallaudet University Press, 1993).

5. Bernard Mottez, "The Deaf-Mute Banquets and the Birth of the Deaf Movement," in *Deaf History Unveiled: Interpretations from the New Scholarship,* ed. John V. Van Cleve (Washington, D.C.: Gallaudet University Press, 1993), 36.

6. Harlan Lane, *When the Mind Hears: A History of the Deaf* (New York: Random House, 1984), 108.

7. Sarah Porter, "Society and the Orally Restored Deaf-Mute," *American Annals of the Deaf* 28 (1883): 186–92.

8. George Veditz, "The Genesis of the National Association," *Deaf-Mutes Journal,* 62, no. 22 (June 1, 1933).

9. A. G. Bell, "Teaching the Deaf and Dumb" (statement before the House Appropriations Committee [1889]) Bell Papers, Gallaudet University Archives, Washington, D.C.

10. A. G. Bell, "Memoir upon the Formation of a Deaf Variety of the Human Race" (paper presented to the National Academy of Sciences, New Haven, Conn., November 13, 1883), Bell Papers, Gallaudet University Archives, Washington, D.C.

11. E. M. Gallaudet, "Values in the Education of the Deaf" (paper presented at the Seventh Biannual Meeting of the Conference of Superintendents and Principals of American Schools for the Deaf, Colorado Springs, August 1892).

12. 34 CFR, §300.550., Individuals with Disabilities Education Act, 1997.

13. Ibid.

14. W. Davis, "The Regular Education Initiative Debate: Its Promises and Problems," *Exceptional Children* 55 (1989): 440–46.

15. Gallaudet Research Institute, *2001–2002 Annual Survey of Deaf and Hard of Hearing Children and Youth* (Washington, D.C.: Gallaudet Research Institute, 2002).

16. Claire L. Ramsey, *Deaf Children in Public Schools: Placement, Context, and Consequences* (Washington, D.C.: Gallaudet University Press, 1997).

17. Padden and Humphries, *Deaf in America*, 9.

18. Ibid.; Harlan Lane, Robert Hoffmeister, and Benjamin Bahan, *A Journey Into the Deaf World* (San Diego: DawnSign, 1996); and Ramsey, *Deaf Children in Public Schools.*

19. Margret Winzer, *The History of Special Education: From Isolation to Integration.* (Washington, D.C. Gallaudet University Press, 1993), 385.

Chapter 1: Beginnings

1. Throughout this manuscript, I use the terms *deaf* and *deaf or hard of hearing* interchangeably. I have come to believe that for adults, these terms become self-labels, and there is no clear-cut or universal delineation between the two. Audiologists and educators recognize lines of demarcation that generally say that the person who can benefit from amplification provided by a hearing aid or cochlear implant is hard of hearing, and a person who cannot is deaf. One can look in any number of textbooks for such definitions. However, in my more than thirty years at Gallaudet and in my travels, I have met people who define themselves regardless of such textbook prescriptions. I have met people who have moderate hearing losses, use hearing aids quite well, and also use sign language fluently, who identify themselves as deaf. Likewise, I have met individuals with profound hearing losses who use hearing aids with relatively minimal benefit, may or may not use sign language, and identify themselves as hard of hearing. One can meet two individuals with the exact same degree of hearing loss, and even with the same etiology (cause of loss, age of onset, etc.), and one of these will self identify as deaf and the other as hard of hearing. Thus, I reject the idea that there is an exact line of demarcation based on actual hearing loss that would identify a person as deaf or hard of hearing. Although I had "only" a 50-dB loss in elementary school, and thus would be labeled *hard of hearing* by audiologists, the loss was great enough to render me "deaf" whenever there was more than one person engaged in conversation around me (which was almost always).

2. In March 1988, the Gallaudet University Board of Trustees, against the recommendations of alumni, students, and staff, appointed a hearing person to replace Dr. Edward C. Merrill, the retiring president. When the announcement was made, Gallaudet students began a protest that drew national media attention. It was the week prior to their spring break, and they were prepared to continue their peaceful demonstration for as long as necessary. The "Deaf President Now" protest was joined by alumni and other members of the Deaf community from all over the United States. At the end of the week, the recently appointed president and the chairman of the board resigned, and I. King Jordan was appointed the first deaf president in Gallaudet's long history. Gallaudet students surely enjoyed a memorable spring break after that.

3. Padden and Humphries, *Deaf in America*, 115.

4. To give the reader some identifying information about the participants in the Solitary Mainstream Project, I have used the following: F = female and M =

male. The number following the gender identification (e.g., "83") refers to the year that the individual graduated from high school. This is important because it indicates how many of his or her K–12 years were spent after the passage of P.L. 94–142, where presumably we would start to see some improvement in the "inclusion" experience.

Chapter 2: Lessons from the Neighborhood

1. Ramsey, *Deaf Children in Public Schools*.

2. Michelle Yetman, "Peer Relations and Self-Esteem among Deaf Children in a Mainstream School Environment" (Ph.D. diss., Gallaudet University, 2000).

3. Stanley Coopersmith, *The Antecedents of Self-Esteem* (San Francisco: Freeman, 1967); Erik H. Erikson, *Identity: Youth and Crisis* (New York: Norton, 1968); Erik H. Erikson, *Identity and the Life Cycle,* 2nd ed. (New York: Norton, 1980).

4. J. D. Coie and K. A. Dodge, "Continuities and Changes in Children's Social Status: A Cross-Age Perspective," *Developmental Psychology* 18 (1983): 557–69; J. G. Parker and S. R. Asher, "Peer Relations and Later Social Adjustment: Are Low Accepted Children at Risk?" *Psychological Bulletin* 102 (1987): 357–89.

5. Yetman, "Peer Relations and Self-Esteem."

6. Susan Harter, *The Self-Perception Profile for Children* (Denver: University of Denver, 1985).

7. *Culturally deaf* is a label used to describe deaf or hard of hearing individuals who are involved with the Deaf community. This community includes a pervasive social network that is international as well as national. There are international gatherings in education, sport, history, linguistics, the arts, advocacy and many more. For example, The World Games for the Deaf are the oldest continuing games outside of the Olympics. Founded in 1924 with 133 athletes from nine countries, these games preceded all other Olympics for special populations. Most recently, over 2500 athletes from sixty-three nations participated in the games. In the sociopolitical arena, the National Association of the Deaf and Community Services of the Deaf are concerned with virtually every aspect of the lives of culturally Deaf people, with the possible exception of religion. On local and regional levels, countless volunteer groups organize their own very full leisure calendars for both adults and children.

Within the ranks of the culturally Deaf are the Deaf of Deaf, those deaf people from families that have included culturally Deaf individuals for known generations. Any deaf child who has Deaf parents can be considered Deaf of Deaf. Families with numerous generations of the Deaf presence are considered the core of the Deaf community. It is within these families that the culture has its origins, and this is true internationally. Historically, this culture was passed from Deaf of Deaf to Deaf of Hearing within the residential schools for deaf people.

8. The children of Deaf parents have organized themselves into a nonprofit organization, Children of Deaf Adults, founded in 1983. Its Web site (http://coda-international.org) gives its statement of purpose as "CODA is an organization established for the purpose of promoting family awareness and individual growth in hearing children of deaf parents. This purpose is accomplished through providing educational opportunities, promoting self-help, organizing advocacy efforts, and acting as a resource for the membership and various communities."

9. Paul Preston, *Mother Father Deaf: Living Between Sound and Silence* (Washington, D.C.: Gallaudet University Press, 1994), 65.

10. Ibid., 74.

11. Ibid., 42.

12. Lou Ann Walker, *A Loss for Words: The Story of Deafness in a Family* (New York: Harper & Row, 1986), 21.

13. Preston, *Mother Father Deaf,* 53.

14. Leah Hager Cohen, "Schools For All, or Separate But Equal?" *New York Times,* 22 February 1994, Editorial section.

15. Susan Gregory, Juliet Bishop, and Lesley Sheldon, *Deaf Young People and Their Families: Developing Understanding* (Cambridge: Cambridge University Press, 1995), 2–3.

16. R. C. Smith, *A Case about Amy* (Philadelphia: Temple University Press, 1996), 98.

17. Marc Chatoff is an attorney who lost his hearing during his late college years due to a tumor. He argued the case of Amy Rowley, a deaf child mainstreamed as a solitary, who was denied an interpreter for her public school class. The court ruled that since she was already doing well academically, she did not need the interpreter. Amy is a deaf child of deaf parents.

Chapter 3: A Glimpse at Everyday Life

1. Padden and Humphries, *Deaf in America.*

2. FM systems are one of several "assistive listening devices" used in public schools. In essence, these are systems that can be used by one or several hearing impaired students in a classroom. The teacher wears a lapel or lavalier-type microphone, and the student wears a receiver in addition to their personal hearing aid or cochlear implant. These systems provide a "direct connect" from speaker to listener and thus reduce extraneous noise, such as that from air conditioners, other students, paper rustling, etc. During the 70s and 80s, many systems involved old-fashioned headphones. In modern times, some schools may have systems that are less obvious. The more obvious they are, the more likely the deaf or hard of hearing student will be self-conscious when using them.

Chapter 6: Social Life in Adulthood: The Oasis

1. John Vickrey Van Cleve and Barry Crouch, *A Place of Their Own: Creating the Deaf Community in America.* (Washington, D.C.: Gallaudet University Press, 1989), 92.

2. *Oral deaf* is the label used to describe deaf individuals who do not use sign language, but rather prefer to communicate with speech, lipreading, and residual hearing, often aided by a hearing aid, and nowadays by a cochlear implant. The terminology does not mean that such an individual's speech patterns will be easily understood by any hearing person, although they may be. It rather implies choice or communication strategy.

3. KODAs, or Kids of Deaf Adults, denotes local endeavors where deaf parents organize activities for their young hearing children. The acronym KODAs distinguishes the very young children from CODAs.

Chapter 7: The Best of Both Worlds

1. Signing songs is a common activity for members of the Deaf community, usually by those who are able to use their residual hearing. It involves signing along with a song as it is sung or played. It may or may not also involve translation into ASL and accompanying dramatics. It is a common form of entertainment at Deaf events.

2. Linda Bittner Crider, Ph.D., personal e-mail to author, July 2002.

3. Summer Crider, valedictory address, Florida School for the Deaf and Blind Commencement, St. Augustine, Fla., June 2002.

4. Thomas Holcomb's essay in response to request for life experience, January 2002.

5. Ibid.

6. The first Deaf Way (1989) and Deaf Way II (2002) were international festivals celebrating the Deaf community. Thousands of actors, artists, educators, and activists from all over the world came to Washington, D.C., to celebrate their unity and diversity at these week-long events hosted by Gallaudet University. Deaf Way III is an event all look forward to.

Chapter 9: Children of Our Hearts

1. In this chapter I use the term *Deaf* liberally. I wish to convey that those who would mentor young deaf and hard of hearing children ought to have the benefit of others' experience as well as their own. When deaf or hard of hearing individuals recognize that they have much in common with other deaf and hard of hearing people and strive to learn about such people, they begin the move toward the qualifier *Deaf.*

2. According to the literature written about cochlear implants, these devices better enable certain users to perceive sound than do traditional hearing aids. However, they do not restore hearing or provide the user with "normal hearing." Implant recipients must also receive what some might call an extraordinary amount of tutelage, practice, and training to recognize the sounds channeled through the implant. Virtually all the books written for parents include a chapter (or more) outlining what the parent must do to ensure that the implanted child will actually receive benefit from the device.

One mother's comments are included in John Christiansen and Irene Leigh's book *Cochlear Implants in Children: Ethics and Choices* (Washington, D.C.: Gallaudet University Press, 2002):

> [a speech therapist we see] . . . makes an analogy that receiving the implant is like receiving a load of building supplies on a lot. And in a couple of years you might have a beautiful new house on that lot if you do the work. But, if you don't do the work, you'll just have a load of building supplies. (148).

These authors and others report that learning to use an implant is something that continues for years, and that both children and adults have varying degrees of success with learning to use their implants. It is considered impossible to accurately predict how much success any given child will have. Mary Ellen Nevins and Patricia Chute's book *The Parent's Guide to Cochlear Implants* (Washington, D.C.: Gallaudet University Press, 2002) states:

> Although no one really knows what implant users hear, implants provide more sound for profoundly deaf individuals than traditional hearing aids do. Implants can deliver high frequency sounds that were never available with conventional amplification. What any individual user does with this sound is variable. Children learn to use sound delivered by a cochlear implant over time with varying degrees of success.

3. Beverly Daniel Tatum, *Why Are All the Black Kids Sitting Together in the Cafeteria? And Other Conversations About Race: A Psychologist Explains the Development of Racial Identity* (New York: Basic Books, 1997), 59–60.

4. Douglas Kleiber, *Leisure Experience and Human Development: A Dialectical Interpretation* (New York: Basic Books, 1999), 76.

5. Ellen Gray, "One 'Survivor' Didn't Turn a Deaf Ear to Adversity," *Philadelphia Daily News*, 5 May 2003.

6. Susan Flanigan, "'Survivor' Christy Smith Credits Model Secondary School for Her Personal Growth," Gallaudet University press release, 18 June 2003.

Selected
Readings and
Resources

*Books marked with an asterisk would make a good starting point for busy parents, teachers, and other interested parties.

*Christiansen, John, and Irene Leigh. *Cochlear Implants in Children*. Washington, D.C.: Gallaudet University Press, 2001.

*Crouch, Barry, and John Vickrey Van Cleve. *A Place of Their Own: Creating the Deaf Community in America*. Washington, D.C.: Gallaudet University Press, 1989.

Foster, Susan. "Communication Experiences of Deaf People: An Ethnographic Account. In *Cultural and Language Diversity and the Deaf Experience*, ed. Ila Parasnis. Cambridge: Cambridge University Press, 1996.

Gregory, Susan, Juliet Bishop, and Lesley Sheldon. *Deaf Young People and Their Families: Developing Understanding*. Cambridge: Cambridge University Press, 1995.

Holcomb, Thomas K. "Social Assimilation of Deaf High School Students: The Role of the School Environment." In *Cultural and Language Diversity and the Deaf Experience*, ed. Ila Parasnis. Cambridge: Cambridge University Press, 1996.

King, Susan J., James J. DeCaro, Michael A. Karchmer, and Kevin J. Cole, eds. *College and Career Programs for Deaf Students* 11 (Washington, D.C.: Gallaudet Research Institute, 2001).

Lane, Harlan. *When the Mind Hears*. New York: Random House, 1984.

*Lane, Harlan. Robert Hoffmeister, and Ben Bahan. *A Journey into the Deaf-World*. San Diego: DawnSign Press, 1996.

Mottez, Bernard. "The Deaf-Mute Banquets and the Birth of the Deaf Movement." In *Deaf History Unveiled: Interpretations from the New Scholarship*, ed. John Vickrey Van Cleve. Washington, D.C.: Gallaudet University Press, 1993.

*Padden, Carol and Tom Humphries, *Deaf in America: Voices from a Culture*. Boston: Harvard University Press, 1988.

*Preston, Paul. *Mother Father Deaf.* Washington, D.C.: Gallaudet University Press, 1994.

*Ramsey, Claire. *Deaf Children in Public Schools: Placement, Context, and Consequences.* Washington, D.C.: Gallaudet University Press, 1997.

Siegel, Lawrence. "The Educational and Communication Needs of Deaf and Hard of Hearing Children: A Statement of Principle on Fundamental Educational Change. *American Annals of the Deaf* 145, no. 2 (2000): 64–77.

*Tatum, Beverly Daniel. *Why Are All the Black Kids Sitting Together in the Cafeteria?* New York: Basic Books, 1997.

Van Cleve, John Vickrey, ed. *Deaf History Unveiled: Interpretations from the New Scholarship.* Washington, D.C.: Gallaudet University Press, 1993.

* Winefield, Richard. *Never the Twain Shall Meet: Bell, Gallaudet, and the Communications Debate.* Washington, D.C.: Gallaudet University Press, 1987.

Walker, Lou A. *A Loss for Words: The Story of Deafness in a Family.* New York: Harper & Row, 1986.

Other Resources

K–12 Programs

RESIDENTIAL SCHOOLS

According to an informal 2003 poll of Deaf of Deaf adults with school-aged children, the following are the best deaf schools in the United States (in terms of high expectations, program vitality, rising enrollment, and quality of students/alumni).

Maryland School for the Deaf
http://www.msd.edu/index.htm

California School for the Deaf, Fremont
http://www.csdf.k12.ca.us

Illinois School for the Deaf
http://www.morgan.k12.il.us/isd

The Learning Center (Massachusetts)
http://www.tlcdeaf.org

Indiana School for the Deaf
http://www.deafhoosiers.com

CHARTER SCHOOLS

The following are up-and-coming schools that use ASL as a language of instruction:

Metro Deaf School (Minnesota)
http://www.metrodeafschool.org/index.html

Northstar Academy (Minnesota)
http://groups.yahoo.com/group/minnesotanorthstar/

Jean Massieu Academy (Texas)
http://www.jeanmassieu.com/home.html

OTHER SCHOOLS

The *American Annals of the Deaf* publishes an annual reference guide to programs and services for people who are deaf.

http://gupress.gallaudet.edu/annals

LAURENT CLERC NATIONAL DEAF EDUCATION CENTER
AT GALLAUDET UNIVERSITY

The Clerc Center's Web site is an invaluable resource with links to lots of information, including state-of-the-art articles about current issues in deaf education:

http://clerccenter.gallaudet.edu

College Programs

College and Career Programs for Deaf Students
http://gri.gallaudet.edu/ccg/

College and Career Programs for Deaf Students may also be purchased in book form by writing to

The Gallaudet Research Institute
Attn: Dissemination Office
Gallaudet University
800 Florida Avenue, N.E.
Washington, D.C. 20002

Learning ASL

For a list of colleges and universities that accept ASL in fulfillment of foreign language requirements, see the following Web site:

http://deafness.about.com/gi/dynamic/offsite.htm?site=http://www.unm.edu/%7Ewilcox/ASLFL/asl%5Ffl.html

Or contact Sherman Wilcox, University of New Mexico at 505–277-6353 (V/TTY).

Community and Advocacy Services

CSD (Communication Service for the Deaf) is a growing organization involved with relay services, community-based advocacy, Deaf festivals, and much more.

http://www.c-s-d.org

Interpreters

The Registry of Interpreters for the Deaf is an organization that addresses interpreting issues.

http://www.rid.org/

Other Deaf Organizations

CHILDREN OF DEAF ADULTS

Children of Deaf Adults is a nonprofit organization for adult hearing sons and daughters of Deaf parents.

http://www.coda-international.org/

KIDS OF DEAF ADULTS

Kids of Deaf Adults was organized by Deaf parents for their hearing children.

http://www.coda-international.org/

NATIONAL ASSOCIATION OF THE DEAF

The National Association of the Deaf (NAD), established in 1880, advocates for the needs and rights of deaf and hard of hearing Americans in education, employment, health care, and telecommunications.

http://www.nad.org/

INTERNATIONAL COMMITTEE OF SPORTS FOR THE DEAF (WORLD GAMES FOR THE DEAF)

Competitive sports have long been a standing feature of the Deaf community. Regional, national, and international competitions are held each year. The first Deaf Games were held in 1924.

http://www.ciss.org/

Miscellaneous

ABOUT DEAFNESS/HARD OF HEARING

This is the best Web site with links to everything you could possibly want to know about deafness and Deaf people.

http://deafness.about.com/mbody.htm

DEAF EXPO

Deaf Expo is a consumer trade show that provides information on services and products relevant to the needs of deaf and hard of hearing Americans. It's is a great way to learn about and be around Deaf people:

http://www.deafexpo.org

DEAF WAY

An international conference and festival created by and for Deaf people. The first Deaf Way took place at Gallaudet University in Washington, D.C. the week of July 9–14, 1989. In 2002, the second Deaf Way drew more than 10,000 attendees from all over the world.

http://www.deafway.org

THE LATEST RESEARCH AND BOOKS CONCERNING DEAF AND HARD OF HEARING CHILDREN

American Annals of the Deaf
http://gupress.gallaudet.edu/annals/

Journal of Deaf Studies
http://deafed.oupjournals.org

Odyssey: Directions in Deaf Education
http://clerccenter.gallaudet.edu/Odyssey/

Gallaudet University Press
http://gupress.gallaudet.edu

Dawn Sign Press
http://dawnsign.com